Sahana Smile
A story of loss and hope

Saumil Shah

Cover design by Jodi Monroe

Edited by Susan Seawolf Hayes

Printed in the United States of America

First Printing, 2015

ISBN: 978-0692503287
eBook ISBN: 978-0-692-52171-7

In memory of my beautiful daughter, Sahana Shah.

You are the light in my eyes.

You will always be loved and never be forgotten.

ACKOWLEDGEMENTS.

I do not walk alone on this journey. It is with great appreciation that I acknowledge those who have contributed to the completion of this book.

Thanks to Susan Seawolf Hayes, for many hours you have spent editing my book to help me get my story out.

Thanks to Brook Cundiff for aiding me in putting my jumbled thoughts in my mind onto paper.

Thanks to Jodi Monroe for illustrating the wonderful picture of Sahana that is being used for the cover.

Thanks to Zac Taliaferro for previewing my book and providing me some valuable insight into the mind of the reader.

Thanks to Holly Zerwig, Valerie Lopez, and Yvette Lopez. I wish we could have met under different circumstances, but I am eternally grateful we met nonetheless.

Thanks to my therapist Mary Combemale and to the folks at Compassionate Friends (Leesburg Chapter) for allowing me a forum to speak freely in my time of grief. You all helped give me the confidence I needed to provide my thoughts to the world.

Thanks to my former co-workers at The Boeing Company for all of the support that you gave me during those first few critical months. Words cannot express my gratitude.

Thanks to my countless friends, from those I have known all my life in New Jersey, to my Penn State family, and to all my local Virginians. We may not be blood relatives, but you will always be considered family.

Special thanks to my family on both sides (parents, brothers, sisters, nieces, nephews, aunts, uncles, and cousins). You all have been there since day one. Your continued support is what helps us get through the tough times.

Lastly, I wanted to especially thank my lovely wife Priti Shah. Without your care, there is no book. We are in this journey together and I cannot imagine doing this without you.

Sahana Smile

PROLOGUE.

CHAPTER ONE. Becoming Parents

CHAPTER TWO. You Are My Sunshine

CHAPTER THREE. Sahana to Savannah

CHAPTER FOUR. The Moment Time Stopped

CHAPTER FIVE. The Hospital

CHAPTER SIX. Saying Goodbye to Our Monkey

CHAPTER SEVEN. Home to Virginia

CHAPTER EIGHT. The Funeral

CHAPTER NINE. Advice from Holly

CHAPTER TEN. Home without Her

CHAPTER ELEVEN. The Medium

CHAPTER TWELVE. Our New Normal

CHAPTER THIRTEEN. Work Realizations

CHAPTER FOURTEEN. Visiting

CHAPTER FIFTEEN. Birthday Celebration

CHAPTER SIXTEEN. Dublin, Ireland

CHAPTER SEVENTEEN. Gizmo

CHAPTER EIGHTEEN. Feelings

CHAPTER NINETEEN. Reconnecting with Valerie

CHAPTER TWENTY. Family Vacations and Holidays

CHAPTER TWENTY-ONE. Savannah after the Tragedy

CHAPTER TWENTY-TWO. Taking Sahana to India

CHAPTER TWENTY-THREE. Signs

CHAPTER TWENTY-FOUR. New Beginnings

PROLOGUE.

We all have a story, an adventure through life that shapes us with each step. This is my story – not the one I thought would be written for me but the one handed down to me nevertheless. I share this story with you because I feel compelled to connect with all those people dealt a similar hand by fate.

I hope my journey will be helpful to all who read this little book. Ultimately, however, I write this book for fathers who have known the unimaginable grief of losing a precious child, no matter what age.

Books on this particular subject, written by a man for men, are rare. Perhaps this one will serve as a starting point. I offer it as an invitation to step toward the light, to use heartbreak as a literal breaking open of the heart so your days with your child make you a better person than you were before.

And of course, I write this story because it's not just my story, it's hers as well. If you are a father who has lost a child, I invite you to take up the pen of remembrance by beginning your own journal of your child's life with you.

CHAPTER ONE – Becoming Parents.

Moments, that's really what makes up a lifetime. Sequences of moments stitched together with laughter and tears. Moments, so very fleeting. Then one day the moments simply stop, leaving a void where once there were vivid pictures.

For many, magic surrounds the exciting time when a couple decides to have a baby. For Priti and me, though, frustration and schedules replaced that feeling of magic. All around us couples were getting pregnant; it seemed so easy, but for us it was a riddle, and we couldn't seem to find the answer. We greatly enjoyed birthday celebrations of our friends' and families' children, but along with that joy came a question: would we ever be the ones hosting cake and ice cream celebrations for our own little one?

Every day the news taunted me, fueling my unspeakable frustration. Weekly there were headlines of these horrible excuses for human beings beating their children, killing their children, or in so many other ways destroying their children's lives. These monsters apparently could easily conceive. They had these beautiful miracle children; yet they treated them as trash to be discarded. How could God have blessed them with parenthood, when they clearly didn't deserve the gift? And here we sat, hour after hour, praying for a child to love and adore.

8,760 hours we'd tried for a baby, one entire year of countless negative pregnancy tests. 365 days of high hopes and then let-downs. With no other options, we turned to the medical world for assistance and found ourselves at Shady Grover Fertility Clinic. Despite its being a medical practice, it seemed warm and inviting. Throughout the endless process of tests, schedules, countless instructions and medications, we were lucky enough to be paired with a nurse advocate by the name of Shirley. She helped guide us through the answering of all the questions to make us feel as comfortable as possible.

For the next nine months we strictly followed the clinic's directions. During this period we tried unsuccessfully three cycles of intrauterine insemination (IUI). The process was so very frustrating; we were doing everything the clinic asked of us, and yet month after month the tests came back negative. We finally decided to take a month off for ourselves, to take a trip to Jamaica to unwind and simply enjoy being together. When we returned from Jamaica and our one-month mental detox, we would try in vitro fertilization (IVF). Little did we know then that fate had other plans for us.

I remember the date – December 8, 2012 – as though it were yesterday. We'd spent the most wonderful day hiking with friends. The weather was beautiful, and we were all in high spirits. We enjoyed the Appalachian Trail, visited a quaint winery and enjoyed dinner at a wonderful restaurant. It was after midnight when we returned home, and we were both ready for some much-needed rest. I was alone in our bedroom when the silence of our home was broken.

"Saum, come here!...Saum, come here!" Priti shouted to me from our bathroom.

I smiled to myself – she must need to be rescued from a dreaded spider. But before I could make it to the bathroom, Priti rushed towards me, nearly knocking me backwards. Her entire body shook, hands quivering so severely she all but dropped the narrow object in her hands. Held between her delicate fingers was something I couldn't ever imagine seeing, a pregnancy test with two lines instead of one. We were pregnant.

She was hysterical, tears drenched her beautiful face. I took her in my arms, holding her as close as possible. Tears stung my eyes, which surprised me since I'd never been the emotional type. I was calm, logical, not easily impacted by waves of emotion. However, as my wife sobbed against my chest, I couldn't help but feel relieved. After days upon days of trying, after tests and schedules and doctors' offices, we were finally going to be parents. Parents, Priti and me. And so I did feel amazement and much, much more, feelings I truly had never felt before.

That holiday season was spectacular. During Christmas we shared our joyous news with our immediate families. They were going to be grandparents, aunts and uncles. This little gift was the perfect present to share with family who had stood by us for so many emotionally trying months. This baby wasn't just our gift, it was a gift for all of those for whom we cared so deeply.

Priti's pregnancy was uneventful. She really didn't experience morning sickness, and we were very thankful for that. From various friends and family members we'd heard stories involving bizarre food cravings coming on strong at odd hours, intense morning sickness striking all day long, and constant discomfort for the mother. We were ready for whatever the pregnancy threw our way, but Priti didn't experience any of that. In fact, we didn't encounter even the smallest hiccup of a complication.

We went back and forth for weeks debating whether we wanted to know the sex of the baby. There were so many benefits both to knowing and not knowing. What became the determining factor was that knowing allowed us to plan ahead. Surprise: that's what everyone talks about when they decide to wait until birth to know the sex of their baby.

Finding out would give us the opportunity to decide on the perfect nursery colors, clothes and every other little detail for our precious baby.

The day of the ultrasound to reveal the baby's gender was filled with almost unimaginable excitement. When it was finally time to find out the sex, we had the sonographer write the gender on a piece of paper and then seal the results tightly in an envelope. Our plan was to open the envelope together in our own time. That time didn't take too long to arrive – we only lasted eight hours before we had to know. Wrapped in the joy of the moment, we went to dinner at a local Indian restaurant, celebrating this amazing moment with wonderful food. Tearing envelope open, the slip of paper hidden inside had one word scrawled across it: "Female." We were surprised! These past few months we'd been convinced that our little baby was a boy, at least that's what we thought from our over-analyzing the numerous ultrasound pictures from all of the doctor visits.

When coming up with a name for our sweet baby girl we had one prerequisite: no one else in our lives could have the same name. We wanted a unique, one-of-a-kind name for the one-of-a-kind baby about to join our family. Priti originally came up with the name Suhani (sue-ha-nee). Although it was a beautiful starting point, it didn't quite fit. I just didn't like how it sounded. From there Suhani developed into Sahana, meaning patience. Patience, as in, we had been waiting patiently for her to come into our lives.

As Priti's belly grew and so did our Sahana, we were able to feel our little baby's kicks. It was the strangest and most amazing feeling all wrapped into one. Our girl was an active little one. You could see Priti's belly moving around depending on how the baby shifted her body. Watching the movement of Priti's belly as Sahana squirmed around helped me relate more to the pregnancy because I could physically see the movements. The perfect mother, Priti would talk to her every day, whispering sweet words to our unborn daughter. Talking to her stomach came naturally to Priti, but for me it felt a little odd to be speaking to a belly. Could she really hear me in there?

In June 2013, we took a babymoon to Charleston, South Carolina. Not only was Priti seven months pregnant, but it was our four-year wedding anniversary. We'd heard so many good things about Charleston, it seemed like the perfect destination – a getaway within driving distance. And Charleston did have all of that Southern charm we'd heard so much about. But as much as we loved Charleston with its friendly people, beautiful architecture, and delicious food, we also wanted to take a day trip to Savannah (which was only two hours away). It turned out to be Savannah that had the "it" factor for us. It was love at first sight. From the squares, architecture and the layout of the city to the kindness of its residents, Savannah was absolutely perfect. I'm not sure if I can put into words exactly what we loved about it, but within those city limits we found everything we desired. We left Savannah knowing without question that we would return to this enchanting city. Perhaps one day we would even call it home.

CHAPTER TWO – You Are My Sunshine.

There is a very strange difference between becoming a mother and becoming a father. You see, Priti became a mother the moment the pregnancy test was positive. She had a beautiful maternal glow about her from that moment on. In that instant, she changed. For me, fatherhood wasn't real yet. It's hard feeling you are the father before the child comes into the world because the connection to the baby doesn't form until you can see her and hold her. I wasn't the man who talked a great deal to the baby through Priti's stomach, but the moment Sahana came into the world I couldn't get enough of her.

In the early morning hours of August 14, the day before our little girl was born, Priti woke up feeling contractions. They came and went, on and off, so we thought for sure that that day was the day. After a few hours of contractions coming and going, they stopped all together. It was a false alarm – there would be no baby today.

The next day started out much the same. Again, on August 15 around 4:00 a.m., Priti awoke feeling the same contractions. Just as on the previous day, they came and went. Priti decided to take a warm relaxing shower to see if the contractions would go away. This time, they continued. Soon after her shower we began timing her contractions, and all the while they grew stronger. It was easy to see that Priti was in a considerable amount of pain.

As the contractions came closer together and the pain increased, I knew we shouldn't wait too long making the drive to the hospital. It was rush hour, and in Washington, D.C. during rush hour, traffic is notoriously bad. Knowing our luck, we would be one of those couples who couldn't make it to the hospital in time and would have to have the baby on the side of the highway. I have many skills and talents, but birthing a child is not one of them.

Around 8:00 a.m. we made a phone call to our doctor, who suggested we come to the office to confirm that Priti was in labor and that labor was proceeding normally. It was only a 25-minute drive to the doctor's office; after arriving, it only took five minutes to confirm that it was time to go to the hospital. After another 25-minute drive to the hospital and time spent checking in, it was nearly 10:00 a.m. before Priti was in her hospital bed.

Priti had always said that she would like to have an epidural (to provide pain relief, as opposed to anesthesia, which results in a complete block of any feeling), but she wanted to feel the labor first. However, there comes a point during the birthing process where an epidural is no longer an option for the mother. I'm not sure exactly when that point is because Priti never got there. She lasted about 20 minutes in the hospital before she gave the go-ahead for the epidural. We were both thankful for the epidural. Once the epidural kicked in, she was able to relax a little more.

The entire birthing process was surreal. I wanted to do everything I could to help, even though I wasn't sure exactly what I could do. My job was to help Priti with whatever she needed. I gave her words of encouragement, although I had a feeling I wasn't exactly great at that part of my job. I can say, though, that she never ran out of water or ice during labor, because I made sure her cups were always full. After a bit of time, Priti got the hang of when to push and when to rest. Once she figured out the timing of labor, things went much more smoothly for her.

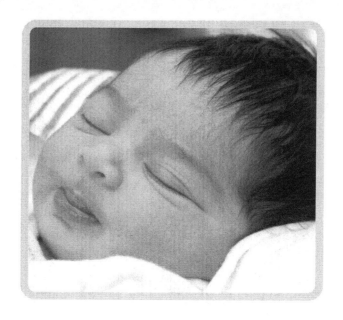

Then the moment that for so long I wasn't sure would happen, did. Sahana came into the world, all thick dark hair and chubby cheeks. Closing my eyes now, I can still see those adorable cheeks – the thought makes me smile. That moment, the hair, the cheeks, that's when I felt it. In that moment I knew that she was ours, our miracle, what we'd wanted for so very long. It was love at first sight. The doctor quickly gave Sahana to her mother, and for a time the three of us held each other. Time seemed to stop around us, there in each other's arms as we became a family. After a few minutes, the doctors took

Sahana to the weighing table, and I followed. Sahana then gave out a big cry, and I thought, "Welcome to the world!"

As things settled down, we had Sahana all to ourselves, quietly watching her chest rise and fall as she slept. We'd heard stories of babies who slept for only an hour or two at a time – a daunting thought. But for that first night, our daughter slept for four hours. We checked on her every hour waiting for her to wake, but she happily kept sleeping. Around 2:00 a.m. she woke up, and it was time for her first diaper change. Priti was exhausted from a day of hard work, so I assured her I would handle it. Big mistake. I was a total rookie, and it showed! I opened the diaper and was shocked: how was I supposed to clean up all of that with a single box of wipes? Surely for such a mess at least a couple of boxes of wipes would be necessary. Such a large mess for such a little being. I was at a loss, and Priti ended up doing the diaper change for me. Sahana 1, Daddy 0.

I was hooked instantly. Being married, I have known what it meant truly to love someone, but at that moment, 7:46 p.m. on August 15, 2013, love took on a different meaning. Looking into Sahana's big brown doe eyes, I melted, a wash of emotions nearly buckling my knees. She was perfect, a beautiful creation more than worth the wait.

The day we brought her home from the hospital was the perfect day with perfect weather. It was a day filled with bright sunshine and warm breezes, a day very much like the day she was born. I checked the car seat once, checked it again and then triple-checked it, just to make sure I had installed it correctly. I have always been a good driver, receiving only the occasional speeding ticket, but on the ride home I became a model example of driver safety. I came to a complete stop and waited extra time to make sure everyone in the intersection had come to a complete stop. At corners I turned the blinker on ahead of time so everyone would know exactly when and where we would be turning. The speed limit was no longer flexible – whatever was the posted limit, that was the exact speed I would drive and no more. Needless to say when we arrived safely at home, and I parked the car and took Sahana in the house, I breathed a lot more easily.

The days and months that followed were like none other in my life, before or since. Every day was a new adventure filled with the light of our amazing little girl. To say she hated her crib was an understatement. She was a girl who knew what she wanted, and she wanted to be close to her mother and me. So she spent her nights peacefully snoozing close to us, either snuggling into one of our shoulders or in her pack-and-play. In amazement, I found myself watching her sleep for hours on end, memorizing every detail about that perfect little creature. She liked to sleep with both hands behind her head, always as comfortable as possible. When she slept close to us, she would take hold of one of our fingers and not let go. She rolled around in her sleep so her head ended up on my side and her feet rested squarely in her mommy's mouth. In the early morning hours, before it was time to get her ready for daycare, she would fart in her dream world. It would make me laugh every time I heard it. I loved all these moments watching her sleep, and with every cute facial expression, she wrapped me even more tightly around that little finger of hers.

Sahana never cried when a stranger approached; instead, each person she met made her laugh or at least smile, as if she had somehow met that soul before she even made it to Earth. She radiated a special warm energy from birth and bestowed it generously on every person she met. Everyone was like a beloved family member to her.

The world was a bright and magical stage for our little monkey. She constantly entertained those around her with her laughter-inducing antics. If she wasn't making slobbery-lipped raspberries, she was creating adorable baby words like "aboo" and "dada." Her own sneeze would cause her to erupt in fits of laughter, sparking laughter again from those in the room.

However, if her "Dada" (Grandfather) sneezed, she would startle or even cry, as she did the first time her aunt fake-sneezed.

It was this sunshiny personality that made her such a hit at Bean Tree Learning Center. From her first day at daycare on January 2, 2014, she was ready to conquer the world. She made friends with countless children, and her teachers adored her from the very beginning. It was important to us that Sahana have the very best in child care while we were away at work, and Bean Tree provided our family with exactly what we sought. Within their walls the attendants cared for our little girl with the love and attention of an extended family, which we appreciated greatly. Her days were filled with playtime and buggy rides. Her creativity grew daily. She even invented a "Tease Mommy" game, which consisted of Sahana reaching out for her mommy and then jumping back into the teacher's arms at the very last second. Sahana's own antics cracked her up!

Sahana was always excited to see what her days at Bean Tree had in store for her, embracing this adventure as she did all else, with an infectious smile. After work I would race to pick her up, excited for much needed Daddy and Monkey time. We would stroll the path by our home after daycare, enjoying the sights and sounds of nature, but mostly just enjoying our time together.

Whatever she was doing, Sahana wanted it jam-packed with fun. Slowing down wasn't an option for her. She woke up chatting away to her hands and her binky, starting her day off with enjoyment before getting up and around. She loved games, even if only with herself, passing a great deal of time playing peek-a-boo with herself using a blanket. Together the three of us played "Where's Daddy?" throughout the house, laughing together as a family. I'm not sure who loved family games more, Sahana or the two of us. She would get so excited when Mommy played hide-and-go-seek by quickly hiding and reappearing from behind my back. Games of tickling her armpits would make her bubble over with fits of laughter. When she wasn't playing games she was playing with toys.

Bouncy seat was go time – every time she was in it, she was ready to take off. In her horse jumperoo, we would have to put a pillow under her feet because without it she couldn't reach the ground to give herself a good, bouncy send-off.

She would bounce and bounce with all of her might, then lift her feet up so she would bounce on her own. Then she'd repeat again and again, laughing the entire time. She loved toys, loved them. Everything from the barn doors and phone on her walker to her Baby Einstein music toy. She would press the button on her Baby Einstein and then put the toy up to her forehead, watching the colorful lights blink. She wanted to enjoy as much time with all of her toys as she could. It was the end of the world if one of her favorites was ever taken from her.

Sahana was a force of nature, never letting anyone stand in her way. When her mommy put her in the playpen, Sahana would bounce up, excited for playtime. She would scoot around in circles on her butt as if there were somewhere she had to go or something she wanted to grab. She hated wet and dirty diapers but didn't have time to lie still during a diaper change. Less than halfway through a diaper change, she was over the experience and rolling around, ready for her next adventure. When the TV was on and we weren't watching Mickey Mouse Clubhouse, she would drop everything to stare in amazement at every single car commercial. Her days were filled with trying to get her toes in her mouth, inspecting her toys, and getting tickled under her right armpit. She was a bundle of energy, always moving, participating wholeheartedly in whatever she was doing at the moment.

With a little one playing so hard day in and day out, she developed a monstrous appetite. When she wanted to eat, she wanted to eat now and she loved to eat, enjoying countless "milk comas," that is, a happy sleep induced by milk, with her pudgy hand wrapped around her mother's finger or mine. In her eyes there was no worse thing in the world than to have her bottle either empty or taken away from her. Often we couldn't get the next bite of food on her spoon before she held her mouth open waiting for the next spoonful. She would eat almost anything except peas; those, she wanted absolutely nothing to do with!

Bath time, oh bath time. It's hard to slow down a busy social butterfly for something as trivial as a bath. However, she tolerated bath time as long as she could sit up, because that meant additional playtime with her bath toys. If she had to lie down for bath time, there would be a strong battle of wills. After bath time she would giggle and giggle as Mommy blew in her ears to get out any tiny water droplets. She would relax and smile as we massaged lotion across her skin, making her smell nothing short of sweet perfection. There are still times I think I can smell that scent.

She became my little partner in crime from her first diaper change at home, which required not one, but 10 baby wipes to complete. If I didn't grasp the concept of changing diapers with fewer than 10 wipes, we would have had to mortgage our home to cover my diaper wipes habit. It was little moments like that, something as simple as a diaper change, which reminded me of how lucky I was. With each breath of fresh air (no pun intended) she breathed into my life, I grew even more hooked.

I looked forward to every second with Sahana. In the morning she would take her tiny little hands and hit the top of my head, trying desperately to grab my short hair in order to wake me up. We spent the weekend mornings watching "Criminal Minds" while Mommy enjoyed some much needed extra sleep. Our weekend routine went something like this: she'd wake me up with a hair pull around 7:00 a.m., and we would sneak out of the bedroom for a diaper change. Then we would enjoy some breakfast, have another diaper change, and settle into the couch to watch "Criminal Minds" and round it all out with a nap. She would usually wake up just in time to see Mommy come downstairs.

Even at the grocery store, it was Monkey and me. When Mommy had to run into the grocery store for a few items, Sahana insisted we drive around the parking lot to give her a more panoramic view of the world around her. Afternoons after Sahana returned home from daycare, she and I enjoyed walks together along the path, quiet time enjoyed greatly between the two of us. No matter where we were or what we were doing, Sahana had the ability to make the worst day become the very best day.

As much as Sahana was my partner in crime, she was also a total mommy's girl. Sahana and her mommy were the best of friends. Priti was the perfect mother to our little girl. From the second we knew Sahana was coming into our lives, her mother adored her. Priti felt blessed and honored to be called Mommy. When Sahana slept or napped, her mother loved nothing more than to watch her sleep. The bond between mother and daughter is one that words can't describe. It's the touch a mother has when her daughter nuzzles into her for comfort that best describes the closeness this pair felt from the very beginning. Sahana loved to bump foreheads with her mommy and would giggle. Sahana looked so safe and content snuggled against Mommy's shoulder, protected by the best mother a girl could ask for. Watching my girls together filled me with such joy, I knew there wasn't a luckier man in the world.

I love Priti, but loving Sahana took me to an entirely new level. No matter how bad a day I had, seeing her or holding her made my day different. I'm no different from any other father of a daughter. In having this precious little thing you realize there is something bigger and more important than yourself. Every decision that used to be so inconsequential now holds significance. It used to be just me. Then it was Priti and me. Then it was the three of us.

After Sahana was born, I started to think about what would happen if something happened to me. How would Priti take care of Sahana? How would Sahana be without her dad? I became consumed with worry about her future. I found work trips to different cities less enjoyable. Previously, I would have said, "Sign me up! If you need me to go to Phoenix, I'll go." After all, I loved to travel. But after Sahana came into my life, I developed a little reservation about traveling. What if something happened? When I was on the trip, I wanted to get home as soon as possible. I missed my family, who meant more to me than any trip.

CHAPTER THREE – Sahana to Savannah.

In May we decided to take Sahana to the place we'd loved so much when we were expecting her – Savannah. The city was so beautiful and so filled with culture, we couldn't wait to re-explore the streets with Sahana in arm. We loved the visit so much the first time, we had to come back.

Walking through the streets enjoying the sights, we decided to have lunch at an amazing rooftop bar. We'd visited this place before during our first vacation to Savannah. The view high atop the roof was breathtaking, and we found ourselves just as amazed with the view this visit as we were our last. From the rooftop you could enjoy views of the large cargo ships leaving the port. With Sahana we found the perfect seat at a table just off the balcony. From the moment we arrived, everyone took notice of Sahana. We could hear people commenting on how beautiful she was, admiring her long beautifully thick eyelashes.

Our waitress was very kind, spending an enormous amount of time at our table talking about Sahana. At the table next to us sat a family of four whom we quickly befriended. They too had been taken by Sahana. The family was so easy to talk with, Priti began talking to the mother at the table about potentially moving down to Savannah. The women's face lit up as she explained that she had done the same thing, moved to Savannah from New York. The two mothers hit it off, exchanging phone numbers before our lunch was over.

The couple even offered to help us locate places to live when we officially decided to move to the area. They knew firsthand how tough it was to start over in a new town, and they wanted to help any way they could. Looking back on this encounter, I can't help but ponder if they wonder about us now – if they ever ask themselves what happened to that happy family with the chunky-cheeked little girl.

After one of the best lunches in my memory, we enjoyed walks through some of the amazing parks that Savannah has to offer. The day continued to be beautiful as we walked along Savannah's park paths, enjoying the squares, parks, tall trees and blooming flowers. It was on the walk that we took a picture with Sahana at Forsythe Park. I can close my eyes and see this image burned into my mind. We stood together, Sahana in Priti's arms, me right next to them. Behind us a wrought iron fence and then a massive white fountain spraying water into a pool. I smiled, Priti smiled, but our little Sahana

41

had a rare serious face. Was it possible that she sensed something to come?

Our walk complete, there was only one thing that would make this day better: ice cream. In Savannah there's only one place to go for great ice cream, and it was worth braving the lines at Leopold's to get it. The lines were always long there, but no one acted as though they minded the wait time. We waited what seemed like forever to order and get our ice cream, when we finally did, there was an open table in the back of the shop. Sahana was beginning to get tired after a day filled with such excitement, but she sat enjoying the scenery around her. While she watched the world go round, Priti and I enjoyed delicious ice cream, on the perfect day.

The thing about last moments is that often we don't know while we are doing them, that it will be for the last time. Priti and I side by side pushed Sahana in her stroller, now working our way back to the hotel. As we enjoyed the sights and sounds of River Street, we came upon a festival. A band played cover music, we listened for a while, allowing time for Sahana to enjoy the melodies and the gentle breeze coming off the water. She was a baby who loved music. As we walked and enjoyed the surroundings, countless people commented on how adorable Sahana was. I felt honored to be her father. Priti even joked that with all the compliments, perhaps we should consider introducing Sahana to the world of baby modeling.

As we made our way along the dock, I took our little princess out of her stroller and held her so she could look over the railing. I remember thinking to myself, "Don't stand too close to the edge...." Later, as we worked our way through the festival, we found a vendor creating names out of wire, and we decided to have Sahana's name created from wire. This is the last thing we did as a family.

CHAPTER FOUR – The Moment Time Stopped.

After a fun-filled day outside, I was getting tired and suggested to Priti that maybe we should head back to the hotel. Sahana was a little tired too, so Priti held Sahana for the walk back to the hotel. When we returned to the hotel, we found a wonderful treat waiting for us. Because the hotel was hosting a ballroom dancing competition, the halls were filled with dance teams rehearsing their numbers. Sahana and Mommy ventured out onto the balcony to watch the dancers work on their routines. Sahana seemed really to enjoy the graceful movements of the dancers. I left the two on the balcony and returned to our hotel room for a moment.

This is when I heard it.

The sound that in my entire lifetime I will never be able to banish from my ears or erase from my memory – a loud pop as though someone had dropped a bottle onto the floor. In that moment the world began to rotate in slow motion, and for the longest breath imaginable, time simply stopped. It was as though all the air had been sucked not only out of my lungs, but from the entire room. A sickening feeling in my stomach told me that it was no dropped bottle.

In that moment Priti's beautiful face grew long, her mouth gaped wide as the loudest scream I've ever heard exploded from deep within her. Priti's eyes were wide, terrified – in the blink of an eye Sahana had escaped her loving mother's grip. Our beautiful daughter had lunged forward, throwing herself out of Priti's arms and onto the lobby floor.

The lobby floor five floors below.

I realized quickly, though my brain didn't exactly accept the knowledge, that Sahana was no longer in her mommy's arms. Priti bolted from the balcony, arms empty, screaming from our room into the hotel hallway. I ran after my wife, following her agonizing screams, but then doubled back, realizing we would need our hotel room key to access the elevator. I raced back to our room, grabbed the key, muttering, "Oh my God, oh my God, oh my God." As I came back to the elevator, I found Priti on all fours sobbing. *"How could I have been so stupid!"* she repeated.

Through the glass walls of the elevator I watched a crowd form around Sahana. I couldn't see our little girl, but I knew she was there. I had no idea what to expect as the elevator doors opened and Priti and I raced across the lobby. Shock rocked Priti's body, bringing her down on all fours when she reached the crowd surrounding Sahana. With knees and palms against the tile of the lobby floor, Priti began to scream uncontrollably. I forced my way through the crowd to Sahana's side while a man performed CPR on her.

"Is she breathing?" I asked.

.

A woman, whom I will later know as Valerie, asked, "Are you her father?"

I nodded yes, and she moved aside, allowing me to get right next to Sahana. I took my daughter's hand – how small it was within my own! I told her that I was right there, and that I wasn't going anywhere. I surveyed her body and could see no blood or anything that appeared to be broken. A small amount of dirt surrounded her from where she'd hit flower pots during her fall. I whispered to her that she was going to be okay, that she *had to be okay*. I talked to her still body until the paramedics arrived.

In the horror that unfolded that afternoon two good Samaritans stepped forward to give us a gift of extra moments with Sahana. Valerie, a mother from Texas, didn't hesitate to kneel by Sahana's side whispering her words of support. Valerie was there for our daughter, making sure that she was never alone. Alongside Valerie was a Duke University nurse named

Randy who rushed to Sahana's side, giving her CPR until the ambulance arrived.

The events of the evening from Valerie's perspective

I'm in town for a professional committee meeting which wrapped up around noon. After walking the streets of Savannah in the thick southern heat, I decide to get ready for dinner. During dinner I remember a few gifts I still need to purchase for friends and family in Texas. After browsing in the hotel gift shop, I make my purchases, completing my transactions at 8:38 p.m.

As I leave the hotel gift shop, I hear a loud clatter behind me. Looking over my shoulder, I see a broken planter with bits and pieces of plants everywhere. I turn towards the main desk to let them know someone has knocked plants off the upstairs balconies. But I never get to speak those words. Before a single sound can escape my lips, I see the shock on the face

of a nearby woman as she shouts, "It's a baby! Call 911!"
Sahana had fallen just after I turned to tell the front desk about
the planter. When I turn back towards the planter again and
see Sahana, I too scream, "Call 911!"

Randy rushes with me to reach Sahana. I have no idea what
to do because Sahana isn't moving, but Randy begins to
coordinate CPR on Sahana with the help of a lady standing
by. Randy gives chest pumps, the woman does mouth-to-
mouth. They focus intently on getting Sahana to breathe. In
this moment, watching the two work in tandem to save this
precious life, I know I need to take a CPR class myself. As the
two work, I hold Sahana's head still. A child Sahana's age
could wake up wiggling about, and I dedicated myself to
preventing any spinal cord damage when Sahana did wake
up. So I hold Sahana's head still with both of my hands.
Sahana's hair is soft and utterly black; her face is lightly
sprinkled with soil from the planter. Although Sahana's eyes
are open, she is not interacting at all with the world around

her. Lying on the tile in her beautiful pink dress, Sahana doesn't cry, and I could see no blood from the trauma. I felt absolutely nothing unusual while holding Sahana's head to suggest she had fallen at all.

As Randy and the woman administered CPR to Sahana, I hear Priti screaming upstairs. Her desperate, agonizing cries continue in the background until they erupt right behind me. Still holding Sahana's head, I turn just as Priti crumples to the ground. To everyone's relief, CPR is successful, and Sahana starts breathing. Sahana's feet are bare, and Randy is tickling them. When I ask him why, Randy explains it is a way to test if Sahana still has movement in her legs. She wiggles her legs, and everyone is relieved that something positive has been accomplished in the midst of something awful. As I turn, I see two additional people tell Priti that Sahana is breathing and she is alive. These people tell Priti to please come hold Sahana's hand to be near her, but Priti is in too much shock to move.

All attention then returns to Sahana, trying to keep her still because she is still wiggling her legs, and they don't want her suddenly to start kicking. A man is standing behind me, and I ask him if he is the father. "Yes," he says, and I ask him to hold his daughter's hand and talk to her. Even though I have no medical training, I know in my heart it is important for a child who suffers such a trauma to hear her parent's voice and to feel the touch of the parent. I watch him and his wife as the father speaks to his daughter, gently asking for "Bucca" (Sweetie) to stay with him. It is at this point that the little girl becomes Baby Bucca to me, and I don't learn her real name – Sahana – until the following Sunday.

As time passes in the lobby, I continue to hold Sahana's head while I talk to her and hold her hand. Then suddenly the EMT's are there, and they sweep Baby Bucca away with them.

When the paramedics were ready to go, they told us only one person could accompany our little girl in the ambulance. Priti was desperate to stay by Sahana's side, so the policewoman who talked to me about the accident offered to drive me to the hospital.

The ride to the hospital was a blend of screaming police sirens and raw shattered emotion. The police car took the lead, clearing the way for the ambulance and Sahana, close behind us. The policewoman who drove the car I was in did her dead-level best to get me to the hospital as quickly as possible. She shouted at drivers to get out of her way, completely frustrated that it took so long to drive five miles. We must have been driving 90 miles an hour, but the drive felt like hours dragging by. As the policewoman drove through traffic, I gripped the cage dividing the police car to keep myself from sliding side-to-side in the back of the car. My heart begged for Sahana to hold on. I didn't want to lose my little girl, but if something did happen to her, I wanted to be by her side. I didn't want my daughter to leave this world without me there next to her.

Through the traffic, the honking and shouts of frustration at drivers, the policewoman constantly counselled me, giving words of encouragement, helping to hold together the shreds of my fraying emotions. She assured me that the hospital had only the best doctors who provided exceptional care. When we arrived at the hospital, the policewoman shouted, "Go, Go!" I left the police car and watched briefly as Sahana's small body was whisked into the hospital.

Priti approached me at the hospital, a pale ghost of her former self. My wife, so full of passion and confidence, seemed so small to me in this moment. She looked defeated. I couldn't even find the words to comfort my wife when all I wanted was to hold my family close against me, protecting them from all harm. I wanted to make everything better, to take her pain away, to fix Sahana... but standing there in the hospital, I was utterly helpless in the face of my poor wife's broken demeanor.

And then: "Take these, I don't deserve to wear them," Priti sobbed, shoving her wedding rings into my hands.

I looked at the rings, tracing them with my fingers. I didn't agree with her, not for a single second. I looked at the woman I married, whom I had loved for so long. Without question she did deserve to wear our rings. I held her, reassuring her that we were going to get through this and that my love for her hadn't faltered in the slightest. I tried giving the rings back to her, but her grief was so strong that she kept returning them to me. Finally I put the rings in my pocket for safekeeping and focused on providing what comfort I could. I wanted so badly to fix the hurt she was feeling, but all I could do was listen.

"How could I be so stupid?" she asked over and over again.

Not stupid, Priti – sometimes unthinkable accidents just happen.

CHAPTER FIVE – The Hospital.

Waiting in the hospital with us was the policewoman who'd driven me so courageously to the hospital. She would end up waiting with us nearly four hours, making sure she was available for anything Priti or I might need. The hospital chaplain also met with us in the waiting room. He asked to pray with us, and though I know he meant well, I simply wanted to be alone. This man so full of faith wanted to share a prayer with me, but in that moment my faith was absent, replaced by insurmountable fear. However, even through our fear we showed the chaplain respect, praying alongside him, even though at that moment, God wasn't really an answer for us.

The second hand on the waiting room clock moved in slow motion. We paced, unable to calm our restless nerves. It all just seemed like a dream. Calling family was out of the question, because our cellphones were left behind at the hotel. So we were left waiting. It was miserable simply waiting

and not knowing. My heart nearly leapt out of my chest every

time a person in scrubs or a white coat came into the waiting

area. Each opened door was the opportunity to hear words

about my beautiful baby girl. There were no doctors, only a

nurse every so often who would let us know that they were still

assessing Sahana. Nothing. Moment after moment of silence

ticked by. Was the lack of news a good thing, a sign that

somewhere within those hospital walls Sahana was still here

with us? Was the lack of news bad news, the delaying of

inevitable heartbreak? All the thoughts running through my

head exhausted me all the more.

At last, word came that the doctors were ready to see us and

that we could see Sahana. My feet were heavy bricks

dragging me down the hallway to see her. My stomach

knotted with nerves. What was she going to look like? Was

she in pain? How could I help my little girl? A father wants to

kiss the booboo and put a Band-Aid on the pain, but there

wasn't a Band-Aid in this world that could fix what had

happened to Sahana.

As we made our way from the waiting room to pediatric ICU

(PICU), I had one question.

"Is our daughter alive?"

The nurse said that Sahana was still alive. We both began to

cry as we entered the room where our little sweetheart lay.

Priti went straight to her side, taking her hand and laying her

head beside Sahana's. How could this be happening? I

watched them, my heart shattering again into a million pieces.

This isn't how things were supposed to be. This couldn't be

happening to us. Only hours earlier we were eating ice cream

and enjoying the park, but now here we were in a strange

smelling room with beeping machines.

An IV went into Sahana's tiny wrist. A ventilator tube went into her mouth and down her throat. Her once bright eyes were closed and her face swollen. Her little arms rested palm side down next to her body. Despite being connected to machines and poked with tubes, she looked peaceful. It seemed that if I tried hard enough, I could pretend she was just sleeping, not lying in front of me fighting for her life. For the next few hours, we just sat next to Sahana, waiting for the doctors to give us any updates. Our sweet little girl really showed no visual signs of the fall. No broken bones, just a little bruising on her arms and slight swollen face. All we wanted was our girl to open her eyes. Those few hours seemed like a lifetime, and all we could do was wait.

It was during this time of waiting that we began to get a few visitors who were privy to the situation. Around 11:00 p.m. police detectives visited us and, following protocol, asked to speak with us about the events of that evening. They asked so many questions, some of which seemed somewhat odd to me, but I'm sure they were simply doing what they had been trained to do. All the questions buzzed around in my head. What happened? What was I doing? What was Priti doing? Did we get into an argument? Was Priti holding Sahana over the railing? That question shook Priti. How could they think she would hold the daughter she loved and adored so carelessly over the railing? Priti would have never put Sahana in harm's way. At some point during the interview Priti began to cry, and answering questions was no longer a possibility, so the detectives agreed to contact us the following day to set up another interview time.

While at the hospital two individuals from the hotel's management stopped by the PICU. I'm not sure exactly what time, but it must have been some time around midnight. The two were very kind, offering their regards and asking if they could do anything for us. I thanked them, letting them know

61

that at the moment we didn't need anything. The conversation was a brief one, and I told them our families would probably start arriving in Savannah tomorrow. They offered to find our families room at the hotel, but since it was Memorial Day weekend, there probably wouldn't be many rooms available. Without hesitation they agreed to set up cots where our families could sleep. They would even make snacks and drinks available to our family to help keep them comfortable during their difficult stay. We will never forget this simple act of kindness. I appreciate greatly everything they were willing to do for my family.

Later that evening and into the early morning, the same compassionate policewoman drove me back to the hotel. The soft voice of the policewoman provided comfort through the disorienting ride back to the hotel although I only heard bits and pieces of those encouraging words. The day had been long, and we needed basic items such as clothing (in our rush I'd left the hotel barefoot) and our phones, without which we were unable to contact our family members. My brain was a swirling scramble of confusion, agony and disbelief. How had such a perfect day, filled with laughter and fun, ended in such horror? How was it possible that my perfect little girl, so full of life only hours before, now lay in a hospital bed fighting for her life? So many questions, questions for which no one in the world could ever have answers.

Standing back in the hotel lobby looking up at the balcony of our vacation accommodations, reality sank in. By "sank in," I mean it slammed into my head with the force of a freight train. Our hotel room was five floors up, well over 60 feet. That fall, that distance, her small fragile body... there was no way she could survive such trauma. My heart begged for a miracle, for some saving grace to swoop in and breathe life back into Sahana. But my head knew the truth, that life is a fragile thing, and once compromised, may slip beyond our grasp in spite of our fervent hopes and prayers to the contrary.

Now, in our hotel room, I stepped out onto the balcony and peered over the edge onto the tiled lobby floor below. For some strange reason, I needed to see, from Sahana's point of view, how far she fell. Then I backed away quickly, gasping quick breaths to calm my racing heart.

I no longer can look over the edge of balconies. Priti and I are now both fearful of heights; we barely even go out on balconies anymore. Even within our own home there's hesitation approaching our second floor loft railing, which overlooks our foyer. Decks aren't so bad for us, I guess because the idea of falling on something soft below, like grass, seems okay to us.

I left the hotel as quickly as I could, eager to return to my family at the hospital. Once in the car, I allowed the GPS to guide me back to the hospital, and when it notified me that the children's hospital was only five miles away from the hotel, I was shocked. On my first trip to the hospital, driving well above the posted speed limit, the hospital seemed more like twenty miles away. I was convinced that the GPS was taking me to the wrong hospital. As I drove, I kept thinking that I just needed to be back with my girls. I couldn't stand being away from Priti and Sahana any longer.

But that five-mile drive filled me with fear. What if something happened to Sahana and I wasn't there for her? I would never forgive myself if I wasn't at my daughter's side when she needed me the most. I would never forgive myself if I wasn't there for Priti when her heart was breaking more than ever before. So I drove, forcing away the panic that crept up from deep within my stomach. The cellphones were dead, no one could reach me, which meant I was clueless for the entire time I was away from the children's hospital. I'm not sure how long it took me to get back to the hospital, but I did feel a small amount of relief as I checked backed in at the PICU. I'd made it back, and that's all that mattered.

No one would ever expect a phone call saying their granddaughter is in the hospital clinging to life. I can't imagine what my mother thought as I tried to explain delicately the severity of Sahana's condition. Talking to my mom I was so nervous, my hands shook as I dialed her phone number and waited for her to answer. I expected her to show disbelief, which I completely understood since I was living it along with her. As I explained to my mother the reality of the situation – that, yes, Sahana was in PICU and the doctors weren't sure what the outcome would be – she asked if the condition was a serious one. After a long pause I finally forced myself to tell her that it was. You can never prepare yourself to hear that kind of news, nor can you ever prepare yourself to be the one giving that kind of news. After that short conversation, my parents would make the long trip from New Jersey to Georgia.

After getting off the phone with my mother, we quickly called

Priti's parents, and my hands shook just as badly this time. I

spoke with Priti's father, explaining the situation; and when I

finished, Priti grabbed the phone from my hand and began

sobbing. As she cried, she begged, "Dad, can you come

now?" It so happened that her parents were traveling as well

and were only four hours away from Savannah. In a heartbeat

they were in their car, racing to us.

Priti and I are lucky to have wonderful family to lean on for

support. If love and support could heal wounds, Sahana would

have been out of bed doing cartwheels. Our family began to

arrive around 5:00 a.m. the following morning and continued

to trickle in until about noon. Seeing each family member was

emotional enough, but watching them in turn see Sahana in

her wounded condition for the first time was nothing less than

heart wrenching. Our families were with us every step of the way, supporting us through each test and every doctor visit, giving us comfort and strong shoulders to cry on. Each family member took a turn spending time in the room with Sahana, Priti and me. The hospital staff was very supportive of our family's presence, even though the family group there to support Sahana was rather large, 11 including Priti and me. We were in it together and everyone was there for the duration. They took turns sitting in the hospital room or sitting in the PICU lounge. The hospital was very kind to our family, checking in, asking if we needed anything. They even provided a room upstairs with a few beds for the duration of our stay so we could all take naps as needed. We were so grateful to have so many people there supporting our perfect little monkey.

During our time with Sahana in the hospital, the hardest part was not knowing. The hospital staff would take Sahana for an MRI or a CT scan of her brain, but then what would followed would be an agonizing time period, perhaps four hours or more, of not knowing the results. Hospital staff told us we would have to wait until the swelling of her brain subsided a little bit before they could conduct more tests. Then we waited some more, followed by another MRI or CT scan. It was a long painful cycle of testing and waiting. We found it hard to focus on anything other than what the next text result might reveal. We were on pins and needles waiting, unable to catch our breath or relax.

Sahana had a talented neurologist by the name of Dr. Baker. He was honest, straightforward, and to the point, which we appreciated. He made it clear that he would give us all the information he had available, good or bad. By trade I'm an engineer, and I live in a world of facts. So I found some comfort in a man who lived in a similar world. I trusted him and knew he wouldn't sugar-coat the situation to spare our feelings. Facts can't be debated, and facts are what he gave us.

Over our next few days in the hospital our family watched as Sahana did not improve. The swelling on her brain wasn't getting worse, but it wasn't improving either. The medical staff was doing all they could. They strove to keep her filled with IV fluids, but she wasn't keeping them in. Then Dr. Baker asked to meet with the entire family in a private room, where he showed us a monitor of Sahana's CT scan. Priti and I sat in front of the screen, our family tucked in close behind us.

Dr. Baker went into detail about what showed on the screen before us. I appreciated the detail, but I was desperate for him to cut to the chase. What did all these details mean for our little girl? Was she going to live? When could we take her home? Sadly, his news was not in our favor: in all likelihood our little angel wasn't going to wake up. It was evident she had some sort of brain damage, though the extent was unclear. Her pupils were not dilating when they were exposed to light.

Her bodily functions were not improving, yet another sign that Sahana was slipping away from this life. We didn't have to say it out loud as we held onto one another crying, Priti and I knew what this meant for our daughter.

Whether it's your daughter or someone else you love fighting for their lives, eventually you tend to gain perspective. As the hours passed in the hospital suddenly the little worries in life seemed so insignificant. Work issues were farthest from my mind. Frustration over sitting in traffic for an extra half hour no longer registered. All those little things I used to fret over, used to obsess about, they really didn't matter. In moments like this, when you hope beyond hope that the person you love can fight hard enough for life, you gain an understanding of what's important in life. Family. Love. Friends. Those things are what really matters. Please hear me when I say this, love the people in your life as hard as you can every single day. Don't let a moment pass, where they don't know how much you love them.

There are life decisions you want to make: where to go for dinner, what to name your family pet, which job opportunity to take. Those are all life decisions as a father you want to decide. Never as a parent should you have to decide whether to take your child off life support. No amount of life experience or textbooks can prepare you for such a decision.

After receiving the facts about Sahana from Dr. Baker, Priti and I went in to see Sahana. It was just the three of us – Sahana, Priti and me. We talked softly to her, telling her that Mommy and Daddy loved her very, very much. Gently, while watching Sahana, I asked Priti if we could talk about what should be done for Sahana. Through her tears Priti agreed to have one of the hardest conversations we'd ever had. It was in that room, looking at our beautiful little girl, we knew we had to let her go. We couldn't fight back the tears at the knowledge that our little girl wouldn't be coming home with us. We wouldn't again see her take off in her bouncy seat or watch her army crawl across the living room. We weren't going to see her move again at all. Our daughter, so full of life, was going to leave us.

"You have our permission to go," Priti spoke softly to Sahana.

CHAPTER SIX – Saying Goodbye to Our Monkey.

Our hearts were heavy, but we had made up our minds. The hospital staff walked us through the process of saying goodbye, bringing in a counselor who provided information regarding assistance we might need after Sahana passed. The hospital offered us a service that casts molds of a child's her feet and hands. We took them up on this offer, having molds made of her left foot and right hand. The foot was done in a classic mold tray.

We tried to do the same for her hand, but her fingers curled up in the mold. So her hand mold was done in a plastic cup, with her entire hand being put in the cup, which seemed to work. We chose her right hand since that was the hand with two fused fingers. At 10 months we would have had tests done to see whether the fingers could be separated; as it was, Priti want to have the mold of this hand because of the hands in the world, it was unique to Sahana.

When we finally got home with the little molds, they each looked like bits of our Monkey. There was so much detail on each mold, from the lines on her feet and hands to fingernails. We are so glad we did the molds. The foot mold was on a flat surface with a raised foot mold. The hand came out to be a 3D mold that appeared so life-like.

Saying goodbye. Nothing prepares you for a moment such as this, the moment when parents have to say goodbye to their child forever. We had each family member speak from their heart to Sahana by themselves. Each person had a chance to hold her one last time. Priti and I were the last ones to say our goodbyes. I took her small body in my arms and cried. I cried out of anger...sadness...frustration.

It wasn't fair. I remember crying and saying, "I want my monkey back." I wanted her to open her eyes and be healthy again. I kissed her, telling her how much I loved her and that I wouldn't give up these nine months for anything. She was our special gift. I kissed her gently on the forehead and lips, saying, "I love you," one last time. Then I handed my daughter to her mommy for the last time. Priti talked to her. She let her know how much she loved her. She sang her the lullaby, "You Are My Sunshine," because she was our sunshine every day of her life. After Priti was done talking to Sahana, I told my brother to get the doctor and let them know we were ready.

Priti, being the beautiful strong mother she is, took Sahana in her arms as I sat by her side. Once the breathing tube was removed, Sahana slowly left us. I watched her beautiful face and tiny fingers that had wrapped around mine so many times. Then I studied the machines, displaying digitally that our daughter was leaving us. Slowly her blood pressure began to drop and her oxygen levels lowered. I looked back at her, memorizing every eyelash, locks of hair, searing in my mind every detail that made her Sahana. Then with a final exhalation of breath, she was gone.

"Why is she so cold?" Priti asked, keeping the blanket tight around her to keep her warm.

Life is fleeting. There one second and gone the next. Moments of laughter followed by uncontrollable moments of tears. The pain of her being so very hurt was real, but the finality of her being gone was impossible to ignore. Her body once so full of wiggles and giggles lay motionless. Her tiny arms lost their youthful glow that she wouldn't come back. One by one, everyone left the room. I was the last one to leave her side, because I had to look at her one more time.

"I love you," I whispered.

After Sahana's passing, there were technicalities to handle, before we could take her back to our hometown. The coroner explained that despite our objections, an autopsy would have to be performed. Her beautiful angelic face was my concern.

Would this technicality cut Sahana's face until it was unrecognizable to friends and family? We were assured only necessary cuts would be made, and great care would be taken in closing the incisions. Then, once back in Virginia, the funeral home would apply make-up to hide the stitches. We weren't pleased, but respected their need to follow protocol.

After talking with the coroner we left the hospital, driving to a nearby hotel where my family spent their nights. Everyone needed rest and food, because for hours we'd been running on adrenaline. It had been a long three days. After sleeping only a few hours, Priti and I decided we didn't want to spend any more time in Savannah. We were ready to go home to Virginia; we simply couldn't be in Georgia anymore.

CHAPTER SEVEN – Home to Virginia.

Since all of our family members, except Priti, Priti's parents, and me, flew to Savannah, we piled 10 of us into two cars and drove straight through to Virginia. Priti, my dad, my brother, Priti's sister and I were in one SUV, then Priti's dad, Priti's mom, my mom, and Priti's two sisters in the other car. One of my brothers stayed in Savannah an extra day to take care of loose ends and be the interface with the hospital, just in case there was a need.

The 10-plus hours on the road were done mostly at night. Priti and I sat in the back of our SUV, holding each other's hand. The vehicle was quiet, no one spoke. As we drove, the feeling plagued me that we were leaving someone behind. Even though my logical brain knew she was gone, my heart was just as confident that we were forgetting someone. Except we weren't forgetting, as we drove all those miles, streetlight after streetlight passing overhead. Every cell in my body longed to hold our daughter. We'd gone to Savannah for a family retreat of fun and laughter, yet we left with a quiet car full of broken hearts. During these hours there were a lot of tears, self-reflection and almost uncontrollable sadness. How had we come to this point? It all seemed like a terrible nightmare, and I desperately wanted to wake up.

Halfway home we all stopped to grab a bite to eat. Sitting together as a family, sharing a meal together, we talked. It was a momentary break from heavy grieving. Within each car unimaginable grief weighed down the heart of each passenger. We drove consumed by our own thoughts, grasping to understand the events of the past few days. However, when we ate together, our grief temporarily lifted.

After hours we finally arrived home, and everyone got out of the cars except for Priti and me. We needed a moment. What had happened was starting to become all too real. Once we went through our front door, we wouldn't be able to escape reality again. In our home there would be no avoiding the emptiness we felt on seeing Sahana's toys, clothes and favorite things. Throughout the car ride we'd held up pretty well, but once we entered the front door of our house, it all came crashing back. The wave of emotion was indescribable. To see her toys and her high chair was overwhelming. We sat down on the couch for a little bit, with family close by outside. Priti wanted to go see her room. I hesitated, knowing it would likely push Priti over the edge. She insisted. Together we went up to spend time in a room that had brought us so much joy; observing her crib, the clothes in her closet and her dresser. It was tough to be in her room, but it was necessary.

We spent the next week simply scraping by, going through the motions and digging for every ounce of effort. All we did, besides lie in bed, was just sit on the couch, which became our central location for grieving. Food was nothing more than a necessity, holding not a drop of enjoyment. We passed time in her room taking in her beautiful scent, holding her clothes and looking at all of her favorite toys – reliving so many past moments, so much laughter and an immeasurable amount of love.

CHAPTER EIGHT – The Funeral.

Before the funeral began Priti and I had some private time with Sahana. Our little angel looked so at peace. As promised, the funeral home did a wonderful job hiding evidence of the autopsy, and Sahana looked like herself. Seeing her inside the casket made for a child, she looked so very small. But she also looked beautiful in the traditional Indian garb that my mom had brought back from India a few months before. The garment was a shimmering light blue silk *chaniya choli* with a short embroidered and beaded top, a bright pink border on the bottom of the floor-length skirt and a matching bright pink sash draped over Sahana's right shoulder. I wish she had had a chance to wear the dress when she was alive, but she looked at peace on her back with her arms over her chest.

Nothing can ever prepare you to see your own child motionless before you – it felt like a scene from a movie, not my life. Bending down and kissing her, my lips became chilled from her cold skin. I knew she would be cold, but I wasn't prepared for how cold she would be. With that I began to cry – we cried, Priti and I, holding one another, completely engulfed in the pain and realization of Sahana being gone. When our family joined us, they too began to cry for such an excruciating loss.

Within Hindu society, funeral rites are an incredibly important sacrament. Hindus look at death as reincarnation, where the soul moves from one body to the next. The soul does so on its path towards Nirvana (Heaven). Death in any culture is a sad occasion, but the focus is on the soul's journey ahead. Therefore, the funeral is a mixture of celebration and remembrance. The body of the departed is cremated, signifying the release of the soul, with the flames of the fire representing Brahma, the Creator.

During the funeral ceremony, Sahana's body was decorated with sandalwood, flowers and garlands. The Hindu priest read the scriptures from the Vedas or Bhagavad Gita. The chief mourner, who is usually the eldest son or male of the family (in this case it was me), lit kindling and circled her body, praying for the well-being of the departing soul.

During the prayer ceremony, the priest spoke to Priti and me, asking a few questions here and there, but mostly reciting scriptures. I genuinely tried to listen to every word he spoke, but it proved difficult. Despite my best efforts, my mind was elsewhere. The ceremony was part of the process, but all I wanted to do was stand next to Sahana. Looking back now, I wish I would have tried harder to focus on the Priest's words. As I have had time to reflect, I realize the significance of the entire ceremony and every ritual we performed.

After the prayer ceremony, a few individuals spoke at the service, including both of my brothers, all three of Priti's sisters, and our really good friend Liz. Each shared their treasured memories of Sahana. It wasn't sad for me to hear them talk about their favorite moments – it actually brought me joy. The hard part was knowing that there wouldn't be any more favorite moments ahead with our little monkey.

To my amazement, Priti wrote a few words about our Sahana. She wanted to let everyone who came to the service know how much we loved our girl. I didn't have the strength in me to speak on this day, and for her to do it was remarkable. My wife, Sahana's mother, is a woman of unwavering strength and love. Even in the most trying of times, she carries herself with complete grace and humility.

Afterwards, Priti and I, followed by the rest of our family, lined up next to Sahana to greet the hundreds of guest who came to pay their respects. The number of people that came out for the service was astounding. People travelled great distances to be there, and we greatly appreciated every single one of them for coming. One by one they stood in line, gave their respects to Sahana, hugged me and then Priti, and worked their way down the line of the rest of our family. Some individuals I knew extremely well, while others I didn't know so well, but one way or another they were all connected to our family. It was wonderful to see them all.

After everyone had had a chance to visit Sahana and our family, the immediate family had some time alone with Sahana to say our final goodbyes. Everyone took turns. Everyone cried. Priti sang, "You Are My Sunshine" and "Momma Gonna Buy You a Mockingbird." As I huddled next to Sahana, I finally lost it. I wept. I'd been able to effect a strong demeanor during the funeral service, but during these final goodbyes, a tidal wave of sadness opened up around me. I lost it. It was the finality of it all, this was it. I told her I loved her and kissed her on her tiny forehead once more. Then we closed the casket for the final time.

In the Hindu tradition, when it's time to go into the chamber room for the actual cremation, only the men attend. With me leading the way, my brothers and three brothers-in-law carried Sahana's tiny casket into the chamber. Both of our fathers came, along with some uncles, cousins and the Priest. We performed a short Hindu ceremony one last time, and then her casket was placed in the chamber. They closed the door. Then it was my turn to press the button to start the cremation process. That was tough, causing me to pause for a few seconds. Whispering, I said, "I love you, Monkey," and pressed the button.

Upon arriving home, as part of the cleansing process, Priti and I went straight to take a shower with our clothes on, thus cleansing ourselves of any negative spirits. Hindus have a thirteen-day mourning period where friends visit and offer their condolences. Hindus believe that the departed soul is acutely conscious of emotional forces received, so prolonged grieving can hold the soul in earthly consciousness. This inhibits full transition into the heavenly worlds. During these days of ritual impurity, family and close relatives won't visit the homes of others, though neighbors and relatives do bring daily meals and take care of necessities during mourning. During this time the family of the departed won't attend festivals and temples, visit swamis, or participate in marriage arrangements. For some this period may last up to one year.

The day after the funeral ceremony we received a note from Holly, a nurse from Savannah Memorial Hospital whom we had befriended. Holly had given my brother a note in Savannah with advice for me to help Priti in the tough times ahead. He chose to give us her note on this day. Holly too had endured the tragic loss of her one-year-old child five years earlier. The note she gave us was first-hand advice on how to work through this loss, advice intended for my wife. Even though I knew the advice was for Priti and for helping Priti through this tragic time, I chose to follow the advice personally also. I know in my heart that it was no coincidence that Holly happened to be working in the hospital the night we went in. Everything happens for a reason, and Holly was meant to be in our life.

CHAPTER NINE – Advice from Holly.

(Although Holly originally sent the advice below strictly for Priti's use, I found it so helpful for fathers in a situation like mine that I decided most of it applied to me also.)

Recommendation No. 1: Keep cards from flowers and service (you'll want them later).

Priti and I will never throw away any cards that are related to Sahana. We keep every single one in a bag with the rest of Sahana's mementos.

Recommendation No. 2: Have someone straighten the house before you go home. Put baby things in your child's room, and close the door. Don't pack up anything.

Before we had a chance to step in the door from Savannah, my sister-in-law came to our house and tidied up a little to try for a balance between having Sahana's things visible and invisible. All of her toys in the family room are still visible but neatly organized in the corner. On our return, her room was just how we left it for vacation in Savannah. Even her hamper itself still has her dirty laundry in it. We are not ready to touch it. The clothes in the hamper are really one of the last things we have of Sahana that still smell like she did.

<u>Recommendation No. 3</u>: Mom and Dad need to go to counseling together, and immediately, if possible.

Priti and I go to individual therapy once a week. We chose our therapist specifically because she experienced the loss of her own child. She's able to relate to what we have been going through. We talk about everything: what we are feeling, how we are managing our days, etc. As skeptical as I was about talking about my feelings to a stranger, this is one of the best decisions I've made in the grieving process.

Priti also found a monthly counseling group,

Compassionate Friends, for us to attend together, which is for

parents who have lost a child. At first I wasn't really keen on

going to this because I didn't really like opening up to a group

of people I didn't know. I had this vision of what it would be

like, a vision developed from watching television. But I'm so

glad Priti found this group. We go once a month. Sometimes

when I'm there I feel like talking, and on other occasions I just

want to listen. Either way, to be around people who are going

through or have been through a similar experience is very

helpful.

Recommendation No. 4: Allow your spouse to grieve. Feelings

themselves are normal, although you shouldn't allow talk of

suicide or causing harm to oneself. If your spouse wants to

talk, encourage that. If not, don't force it.

I try to let her grieve as much as she would like. I usually

let her dictate when she would like to talk, only because I know that is what I want for myself. There were definitely some times when suicidal thoughts came into play on her part, which scared me greatly. However, when I would talk to her or allow her to cry on my shoulder, eventually her dark thoughts would subside. My focus was to be next to her if she ever started to cry. At her side I would ask some questions and if she was ready to talk, we did. If not, that was okay too. I just wanted her to know I would always be there to listen when she was ready.

Recommendation No. 5: Try to keep outsiders informed of the situation (perhaps through a third party) so neither you nor your spouse has to continue to answer the same questions.

For us, this either was not really an issue, or our family and friends did a wonderful job of shielding us from the questions. Having a family member or friend shield us from having to answer the same questions definitely gave us more space to grieve. On the same note, if repeated questions came up, we had no problems answering it. Once you come to the realization that your family and friends are genuinely concerned about you, the repeated questions become a non-issue.

Recommendation No. 6: Have each of you choose one or two of your child's favorite things to hold and keep with you at all times.

I carry her favorite jacket with me everywhere I go. It's a white and purple giraffe cow jacket. It gives me comfort to know that she is with me. Whether I'm at work or going to the store, it's with me at my side. Everywhere I go her jacket is with me, clipped onto my pants. At night the jacket is with me even when I sleep. I also have a personalized bracelet I wear at all times. It is black metal with a silver inscription. It's inscribed with "Sahana Shah 283:13:45" (which represents the Days:Hours:Minutes she was alive) written on the outside and her birthdate "August 15, 2013" written on the inside.

Priti carries around a necklace adorned with pendants of Sahana's birthstone, an angel's wing, her initial "S", and her name. She also carries Sahana's washcloth in her pocket. On occasion, she carries with her a dragonfly token a friend gave for times when she needs some luck. At night, Priti sleeps with Sahana's monkey doll and clutches it tightly in times of need. She rarely lets it go.

Recommendation No. 7: Make sure you each get medication for sleep and to help with depression, should you need them. Monitor your spouse's and your eating and drinking. It's okay to drink more than you eat, just make sure you eat a little each day. (Someone else should control your medication.)

We both went on medication to help get through the days, antidepressants as well as sleep aids. I was a little apprehensive about them, but they really do help. Sometimes our minds aren't ready to process everything, and we need a little bit of help coping. You could definitely see a difference in

Priti after she started taking the medication. She was still

having grief issues, but the meltdowns were fewer.

Priti was able to fall asleep rather quickly at night but was

having trouble staying asleep. I, on the other hand, had

trouble getting to sleep. Our minds would wander at various

times, and the sleep medication allowed us to get some much

needed rest. If we didn't get rest, then we were of no use

during the day, and the endless cycle persisted.

Recommendation No. 8: Make yourself get out of the house

for short drives. Take a shower, anything to encourage a new

"normal" routine.

It was difficult for Priti and me to leave the house, but we

forced ourselves to do it, with encouragement from our family

and friends. Along the path right next to our house we would

take short walks, just the two of us, hoping we wouldn't see

anyone we knew. We weren't ready to talk to anyone.

Generally we did not see anybody, mainly because we would

walk around dinner time. On the walks, we would reflect on the day and how we were feeling. We reflected on the support we'd received from everyone and on the letters and cards we had received that day.

Sometimes our walks took us by a playground, which from time to time reminded Priti of Sahana. This would ignite her grieving process again. At the time, we probably didn't appreciate the walks as much as we should have. What these walks gave us was the gift of time to reflect on the day and just enjoy the beauty of the summer.

<u>Recommendation No. 9</u>: If either of you wants to leave your child's room set up for one month or five years, that is fine. The two of you will decide when you are ready.

We haven't touched her room. Her hamper still has her dirty laundry in it. Her dresser and closet have her clothes in it just as they were when we left. Her bag that we took to Savannah is still packed with her clothes, and it hasn't been opened since we returned. One day we will open it, but it will be on a day of Priti and Sahana's choosing.

Recommendation No. 10: Mother and Father will grieve differently, and that is as it should be.

This advice by far is the single most important advice I've ever received. Priti and I do grieve differently. We learned early on that it was okay for us to differ in our grieving processes. I've seen marriages affected by not understanding this concept, and I knew I didn't want this for us. Some of those relationships ended in divorce, but I can't imagine my life without Priti. I grieve privately or just with Priti. Priti is more open about her grief; she will break down whenever grief overcomes her. I am more aware of my surroundings and want to hide it away a little more.

We have embraced all of Holly's advice and are so thankful to her for sharing her experience with us. Her words of wisdom have been a great help during trying hours.

CHAPTER TEN – Home without Her.

Both sets of parents stayed with us for weeks following the accident. In these days the loss could have either ripped our family apart or brought us closer together. Even after death, Sahana continued to help our family grow even closer. The moms kept busy with cooking and household chores, anything and everything they possibly could think of to help take worry from Priti's mind. The dads worked together on household projects I had lined up for them, the biggest one being renovation of a room in our basement. For weeks our family was there for us around the clock. This is the thing I love the most about our culture: family and extended family are there for you. It doesn't matter how directly or indirectly they are related to you, when you need them the most, they will be there without your having to ask. You can always count on them, no matter what.

After the accident I found myself reading every article I could find about Sahana. I hadn't thought that our loss would make even the local, let alone the national, news. I was looking for information that would help me piece together the events of that day and the days that followed. I knew only what I had experienced, not what others had seen. These differences in perspective and what they meant to our story were brought to my attention by a telephone call from an AP reporter asking for comments regarding the accident. The reporter was just doing his job, which I understood, but there were details in these news stories that were irrelevant. To be honest, we wished we could have gotten through this part of our lives without our full names and occupations, including our places of work, being published. And at one point I had to suspend my Facebook account to prevent third parties from using images of our family without my permission.

Like me, Priti was drawn to the internet to read similar articles. Unfortunately, she also read the comments posted publicly to those articles. The cruelty of the human race amazes me.

How people could write the things they did with no disregard

for Sahana's life or for our grieving family disgusted me. From

across the country people judged Priti in the harshest way,

blaming her for the accident. People speculated on the true

cause of the accident – everything from neglect to intentional

harm to Sahana. How could people who had never met us,

who had no knowledge of the accident, and who simply read a

media report pass such strong judgment?

The comments from these heartless, anonymous people

forced Priti's self-esteem to plummet to a new low. She was

still passionately grieving the loss of her beloved daughter,

and now she felt the harsh criticisms of complete strangers

breaking through the last bits of strength she had.

One particular evening, after she had devoured all the hate the internet could throw at her, I watched my wife closely, scared I might lose her also.

That night I laid awake watching Priti, afraid to doze off even for a moment. My wife was broken, and for the first time since we'd lost Sahana, I was afraid of what Priti might do. It made me angry that people would use words to destroy my beloved wife's ability simply to get through a day.

I myself refuse to validate those individuals who participate in the blame game. For Priti, though, it is not so easy. She was already blaming herself, and all these individuals did was reinforce that tendency. When tragedy involves children, the first thing to be lost is reason. We want someone or something to blame, no matter the cost. People read the story about Sahana, and they simply must blame someone. Priti took the brunt of that blame. Those bystanders believed they would have done something different if they were Priti. In retrospect, we would all do something different.

Before the accident, we passed our time doing whatever the little boss (Sahana) dictated. I would generally pick her up from daycare around 5:30 p.m., where she would greet me with a smile so big it melted my heart. Then I would take her home for a snack or for one of our walks, with her in her stroller. Sometimes she would be so tired from her day of play, she would doze soundly in her car seat during the drive. On these days I would quietly take her inside, turn on the fireplace and allow her to sleep by the warmth of the hearth. We loved this time together, waiting for Mommy to get home from work.

After our loss, I wasn't sure what to do with myself, without my favorite monkey directing the show. Things simply weren't enjoyable anymore. Wasting time surfing the internet was mundane, and watching television had lost its appeal. Listening to music was out of the question because it only managed to fill the hole in my heart with heartache. We were

utterly alone with our thoughts. Upon reflection I am thankful

for this time, though, because it gave us the much needed

opportunity to face our grief head on. Thanks in part to the

drabness of technology, we found ourselves unable to hide

behind it as a distraction from our real task.

And to be fair to Priti and me, we were becoming aware that

we each had posttraumatic stress disorder, or PTSD. Not that

we had been formally diagnosed by a doctor, but it was so

obvious. We both suffered from intrusive thoughts. Priti would

be exhausted from emotionally trying days and would crash

into bed at night. I found myself somewhat functional during

the day, with projects to distract myself from the thoughts firing

around inside my brain. But when the sun set and I lay in bed,

I was no longer able to avoid the ricocheting thoughts. They

invaded my consciousness, blocking my ability to fall asleep.

Even now I have issues with sleep eluding me when the world

is quiet. These sleep issues, plus difficulties with

overwhelming anxiety and recurrent depression surely added up to PTSD.

During this time, I did a lot of reading, online and through books, researching the brain and the effects of traumatic brain injury. I quickly grew obsessed with knowing what my little monkey had gone through. By understanding her condition, I hoped to be able to understand her more fully.

But along with voluminous research and reading, I did a whole lot of nothing. I would find myself sitting, not watching television or listening to the radio, just sitting and looking at pictures of Sahana. In fact, there was a span of nearly two weeks when not a single TV was on in our home. We finally turned on the news so that our parents could feel some sense of normalcy.

Family members and friends stopped by for visits. Drawing from Holly's advice, some days Priti and I would try to go on short walks along the walking path next to our house. This was heartbreaking since we'd walked that path so many times with Sahana. One path took us by a playground filled with children. Seeing them only served to remind us even more what was missing. But the walks, though painful at times, were necessary – we were able to get fresh air, to talk about Sahana and the future, and to reflect on how much support we had received. Sometimes when we returned, we would feel worse than when we left, but at least we were doing something other than sitting on the couch.

During my research on the afterlife, I found that people were able to communicate with their lost loved ones through meditation, which apparently allowed the mind to be more open to receiving messages from those who have passed away. It is simply a matter of raising one's vibrational frequency. It was then that I started my own practice of meditation. In the morning I would go to our living room and load up the 21-day meditation course on my iPad. I guess the whole point of a 21-day period is to build a habit, and it did. It was a three-minute meditation that I found to be very effective. I would meditate in the morning before I started my day, to help with relaxation, to slow everything down and provide me better perspective. I'm not sure if it helped me in my efforts to communicate with Sahana. I wish I had picked up meditation earlier in my life because I definitely could have used the benefits.

If you'd asked me before Sahana's accident about the afterlife, I would have told you I was a skeptic. I was more a person of science than I am now regarding this matter. If there wasn't tangible proof of something, then it simply did not exist. Following the accident everything changed. Sahana had died, but I knew she had to have gone somewhere. It's not possible that this life is just it, there has to be something more. I refuse to believe that she died and simply, poof, ceased to exist. If that is the case, then who cares what we do throughout this life?

I started reading a lot more books on the afterlife. Hearing stories from other points of view inspired me to research and form my own opinion on the afterlife. Slowly I shifted my attention to what the afterlife might be. I believe in my soul that Sahana's spirit is still strong and full of light, somewhere. Her energy, the brightest light I've ever seen, didn't dissipate into darkness. An energy like hers ignites the dark. It's ironic that I didn't really believe in organized religion, but I definitely have converted to the possibility that there is something beyond this life.

Wherever her light is, the travel bag we took to Savannah with Sahana's clothing and other personal items remains intact. I'm not sure what's in the bag, but we aren't ready to unpack it just yet. The numerous toys she played with in our family room are still there, just a little more organized in the corner. We don't want to put them away. We like seeing them as a reminder of her favorite things. Her highchair still sits at our dining table, letting her know that wherever she is, she always has a spot waiting for her at home. Her room is untouched, like big open arms waiting to welcome its baby home. I love this space, I feel so near to her here. I'm not sure when or if we will change her room or unpack her bag. Time will tell, and I'm sure Sahana will let us know when the right moment arrives.

We've compiled all of the pictures and videos taken by friends, family and us of Sahana. As one of the tributes to Sahana, Priti created a video compilation of all of the memories, and I'm so glad she did that. I watch her nine months of life, time and again, through a video montage, 45 precious minutes of her life compiled, held together with giggles and joy. It's so emotional for us to watch through these moments of happiness and realize that the video will never grow in length. A life, so short, summarized in 45 minutes, 2,700 seconds. I want more seconds, I would do anything for even one additional second with our smiling chubby-cheeked little monkey. Though they are bittersweet, I'm thankful for these video clips, and I'm thankful for every single breath I took with my daughter. I am truly a better person because she was in my life.

CHAPTER ELEVEN – The Medium.

After reading a lot of books on the afterlife and seeing signs of Sahana all around, we decided to see a medium. I know what you may think; believe me, we both were skeptical at first. We were looking for anything to reconnect us with Sahana. After talking we figured, what's the worst that could happen? That the medium would tell us stuff we already knew or some general information? If that was the case, so be it. The only thing we would lose would be time and money – both very insignificant in the grand scheme of things. Together, Priti and I decided it was worth the risk.

I spent hours researching the subject on the internet until I came across Monica the Medium. When I reached out to Monica, I purposely did not give her much information, just my name. I was impressed when Monica didn't ask for additional information either. She was careful not to focus on any extra details that might distract from the matter at hand. It was that distancing herself from extra facts that solidified in my mind that she was the one.

Our session with Monica on July 21, 2014 was an hour and a half. When we walked into our reading, the only thing she knew about us was my name, Saumil. When we started, two people came through to Monica together and another followed shortly after. One of the people was Priti's grandfather, and the other was a nine-month-old baby who recently passed, Sahana. Our little girl was coming through.

Sahana kept showing the medium the number "1," signifying the first and/or only. Monica was able to identify the letter "S" and the letter "A" as part of her name. The third person coming through was a heavy smoker, my late uncle. The medium was able to identify the exact date of birth and date of death for each of the people coming through to her.

The medium began to talk about Sahana and the day of her

accident with information gleaned from others coming through

to her. She knew that Sahana had suffered a head injury,

where the incident happened, and that she'd hit things on her

way down. Monica knew that I wasn't with Priti when the

accident occurred. The medium saw that Sahana had chubby

cheeks and big eyes, without ever having seen a picture of

Sahana.

Sahana kept showing the medium her earrings, and Monica

would tell her how pretty she looked.

Sahana was able to show a great deal to Monica. Sahana

remembered having skin-to- skin contact with her mom. She

identified the green glider in her nursery and remembered

sitting in the chair. She enjoyed her time playing under her

play gym and all the times she and I would giggle together.

Sahana even remembered that the colors in her nursery were

pink and cream. Our little angel let us know that she knew her nursery hadn't been touched, and that we could keep it like that as long as we needed. Even now, she was ruling the roost, letting us know how things would be, and looking out for her mother and me.

Sahana let us know that she was always around. She rejoiced in her memories of her time on earth, remembering fondly her loving family. The medium identified "MAR" for Margi's *(my older brother's wife)* home Sahana remembered playing at often. Sahana shared so many memories during our reading with Monica: her love for the flowers from her service, her favorite musical toy, a stuffed animal she slept with. She also wanted us to know that she listens to us talk every single day and that she loved the countless ways we choose to remember her and keep her close to our hearts. So she knew about the garden, the pictures and the jewelry.

Our princess, our monkey, let us know that it was okay to have more children, that she wanted us to have more children and that each of them would have a piece of her. We were told to keep our eyes open for a sign from Sahana soon and that we should pay special attention to anything with wings (butterflies, dragonflies, a white duck). Sahana also made it clear that she wanted us to continue our charitable work. She was so wise, our little girl. Even the medium noted that Sahana was in fact a very old soul and incredibly wise. The medium even encountered strong emotions and goosebumps throughout the entire reading. In all, it was one hour and thirty minutes of confirmation – we knew our little girl was still with us.

Priti's reaction to the reading was profound; she found some closure in Sahana's talking to her via Monica. Priti was riddled with immense guilt about the accident, but after hearing from Sahana she slowly began moving forward. Sahana had told Priti to step away from the guilt. She said it was her time to go and that there was no changing the outcome. If she hadn't left this way, it would have happened another way. Sahana's words really stuck with Priti. After our meeting with Monica I saw a big positive change in Priti and it gave me hope. I saw her able to function a little bit better each day, taking steps forward. The shell of grief that surrounded Priti began to crumble with each passing day. She now understood what I'd already known: Sahana's accident wasn't her fault, it was just a terrible accidental event.

How did I feel about the reading? I'm still a person of science, I wanted facts and reassurances that Monica was telling us things she couldn't find by searching the internet. Some of the moments she mentioned were definitely ones she could grab from the internet, but she said a few things that no one could possibly know, things kept close between Priti and myself. During our meeting Monica mentioned that she kept seeing pictures of Boo from Monsters, Inc. Monica couldn't explain why she was seeing that repeated image, and so at first she was hesitant to mention it. Boo was only a reference Priti and I had for Sahana because of her similarity to the pigtailed cartoon character in a picture we had taken. Monica also mentioned a tattoo in honor of Sahana; I had debated a long while about getting a tattoo in her honor but opted for the black memorial bracelet instead.

I am not really sure what people will think of Monica or our visit with her. I feel confident in the real emotion she relayed while interacting with Sahana. I don't believe her emotion was fake or scripted. Monica was able to express to Priti that Sahana knew the fall wasn't her fault. That when it was her time to go, it was her time to go. That even during her passing she felt no pain, because her soul left her body before she hit the first ledge. If her death hadn't been then in the hotel, it would have been another time soon, another way. Sahana had a clock of life, and it was simply the time for her spirit to move forward. Without Monica, we might never have come to grips with this fact.

There were definite changes in Priti's demeanor after we had talked to Sahana through Monica. I noticed, for instance, that Priti was starting to give herself a little break. Hearing Sahana tell Priti to stop beating herself up, Priti's psyche began to heal. She was still feeling the guilt of holding Sahana that fateful day, but you could see that the guilt wasn't as strong as it had been previously. She no longer seemed to have that feeling of desperation as in the days following the accident. For me, it was a relief. I no longer had daily worries about her harming herself. I felt she would physically make it through this tragedy. Now this doesn't mean in the back of my mind that the thought wasn't there that she could still hurt herself. It was there, but it just wasn't in the forefront.

CHAPTER TWELVE – Our New Normal.

When my eyes open in the morning my first thoughts are of her. Once I get out of bed I talk to Sahana about the day awaiting me, the project at work or the errands I need to run during my lunch hour. It's natural to want to tell her about my day. I ask her to keep an eye on mommy while I'm away at the office and mommy is completing her day-to- day tasks. If anyone can keep Priti safe, it's Sahana. I also ask my precious guardian angel to watch over her beloved family members that are traveling that day and to pay extra special attention to those not feeling well. I ask a lot of Sahana, because I know she's watching over us all wanting to help in any way that she can.

Each morning as dawn breaks at our house I find myself drawn to her room, pulled to be just a little bit closer to the things that belonged to her. I walk in and greet her with a warm hello and kiss her pictures laying on her dresser, because in this place like so many others, I feel her so close to me. It's almost as though I can see her greeting me in return, with a smile that lights up the room.

As I remember her, taking in each item in her room, I venture into her closet or drawers, breathing in her scent from a folded baby blanket or beautiful dress. It's after breathing her in deeply that I'm also knocked over by the intense memories that flood my mind. I've read that scent is the strongest memory reminder, and I strongly believe this to be true. In this space, engulfed in what's left of her, I feel at peace. For just a moment longer, I feel all that much closer to Sahana.

Bedtime for me always plays out the same way. Every single evening I fill Sahana in on my day. I describe my trip to the market or the conversation I had with a coworker. I share with her what I enjoyed for lunch or how terrible the traffic on the highway was. It's the little things I know she cares about, the little things I want so desperately to share with her. I never miss out on my chance each evening to tell Sahana about my day. This time is an emotional time, spilling my soul to a beautiful little girl, who though I know is watching, can't answer back. I find myself flooded with emotions, tears often uncontrollable.

There are three pictures of Sahana that always stay in our bedroom. Two of them are framed images that are nearly life-size and sit on the floor – images displayed at her funeral, images I kiss goodnight, but have trouble talking to as easily as I do to a third framed image. There is a framed picture of Sahana that I hold as I talk to her. Looking into her deep brown eyes, wanting so badly to take her in my arms. Each night when I'm out of things to share, I kiss this picture three times, pulling it near me. I tell her:

"Love you Bucca (Sweetie), Love you Monkey, Love you Sahana."

The darkness of night is a taunting time passed by hours of tossing and turning with a restless mind. The hours tick by slowly, filling my gut with nagging anxiety. I wake exhausted, a zombie stumbling through my day-to-day routine. My day passes filled with groggy action completely void of purpose. I need sleep, but sleep is often the one thing that escapes me. When the day ends and the nighttime darkness blankets the walls, I'm unable to find the comfort of rest. It's a vicious cycle and is unyielding.

Somewhere in the struggling to pick up the pieces of our shattered lives, I needed to show Priti we were a team. I needed to show her I wasn't going anywhere and that we would get through this together: I needed to give back her wedding rings. The rings that she told me she didn't deserve to have back in the hospital in Savannah. For Priti, her feelings of guilt over the tragedy at one point became so overwhelming, she questioned whether she was worthy of marriage. But for me, Priti's worthiness to be married to me was never in question.

Thanks to Holly's advice, Priti and I were both able to find medication to help us through. I find some relief in sleep medication. It chases away my overactive thought process enough that I can find sleep, even if it does take me a while to get there. Even with the benefit of sleeping through the night, I'm clouded by the effects of the sleeping medication. In the months that followed the tragedy, I've switched between countless anti-depressants. I wasn't looking for a happy pill. Not a quick fix. When I found the right medication, it allowed me to stop experiencing the extreme highs and the tumbling lows. It helped me slow down a little bit, decreasing the stress that wrecked my body. It took switching medication to find the right treatment for me.

Along with accepting help from medication, I had to learn to accept help from other people. In letting people in, I was able to open up and express how I felt. Finally I understood that I wasn't alone in this world. There were people right beside me and around the world who had experienced similar tragedy. There was hope that I could make it through this. This is a big part of the healing process. I had to want to let people in. We often reached out to others in need, genuinely wanting to help in any way possible. Sometime people would take us up on our offer, other times they would not. On the flip side, when people reached out to us, they genuinely wanted to help. They were our family and friends. So why not let them help.

The months after Sahana passed, people would ask how we were doing. I wouldn't sugarcoat it. I wouldn't say we were doing just fine. I would be honest. If the roles were reversed, I would want to know honestly how they were feeling, so I was honest with them. There was no hiding what we were feeling, and it was quite therapeutic not to have to speak through a filter all the time. If my friends and family wanted to know what we were up to and how we are managing, well, they would know, and I think everyone honestly appreciated that.

Everyone comes into our lives for a reason; the uncontrollable aspect of life is that we can't negotiate how long that person stays. For us we had nine months of perfection with a precious little gift. She was given a life contract of nine months and filled those days with never-ending love. She brought a completely new perspective. She brought inspiration far beyond her years. Maybe she came into our lives to change our views and give us the gift of insight. Maybe her reason for joining our lives was to teach us about ourselves.

Nine months. It's too short, it's not fair. That is, however, enough time to live a life that imprints on others. I am a better person today because of that little girl. In the days and months since Sahana entered my life I have become the man I was supposed to be. She filled in the pieces of myself that I hadn't known were missing.

Without question I believe we were drawn to Savannah for a reason. Sahana's destiny was linked to that Memorial Weekend in Savannah, and that's why she led us there. Just as with her mother and me, Sahana impacted everyone she touched. Those days in the children's hospital, surrounded by countless staff members, Sahana imprinted on those lives. She was meant to touch those people, and they were meant to touch us. The members of the children's hospital team have brought so much into our lives. Moving forward we will carry those people in our hearts, continuing to keep in touch with them. Our daughter guided us to Savannah, so the city and the amazing people in it will always be a part of our story.

CHAPTER THIRTEEN – Work Realizations.

Going back to work seemed unimportant in the months after Sahana's accident. Sometimes I wonder about what we all are doing here, including outside of work. I struggle daily trying to understand the importance of everyday tasks. Who cares about the lady who just cut you off on your way to work? I don't get mad anymore. Who cares about the gloomy events of the day that seem to highlight the daily news? Does it really matter? Who cares about the endless cycle of political propaganda that inundates our lives? Who cares about the deadlines for the next project? It mattered absolutely at one point to me, but since my return to work, it doesn't matter all that much. There is so much more to life than all of that nonsense. My circle of friends and family is all that matters.

Sitting at a desk, pretending things were normal, didn't seem worth it anymore. The company I work for from the bottom to the top is filled with extremely supportive people. They aren't simply coworkers, they are a second family to me. They gave me free reign to come and go as I was able. Starting back I would work an hour or two every couple days. That grew into working half days on a regular basis, finally developing into working full days while still keeping the flexibility to handle the important items at home.

The amount of direct and indirect support I received from those work individuals was remarkable. I will never forget that generosity. Coworkers offered to donate their vacation, helping to give me additional days off. I didn't know this until after the fact, but it chokes me up every time I think about it. I am surrounded by some of the best people imaginable. Coworkers cried when they heard the news, not just those whom I'd known personally, but individuals who barely knew me on a personal level. That means a lot. As much as employment is a place of work, a career to earn a paycheck, it can be so much more than that. All those people, those selfless wonderful people, are my work family. In the end they have my back, no matter our level of personal interaction. I know I haven't said it enough, but I am so thankful for each and every one of the people within my company. They circled around me and lifted me up when they didn't have to.

My life at work has changed a great deal. Is it a midlife crisis? Is it grief? A combination of the two? I'm really not sure. The petty frustrations that used to grind my gears are a thing of the past. I no longer find myself frustrated with coworkers and by the work projects that need completed. Those minor annoyances seem so trivial now. However, I do have a nagging feeling that asks me if it's time to make a career move. Is it time for me to follow a new path or begin elsewhere? Leaving my current position is difficult to contemplate, because I feel obligated to stay and support my team. All I know is that at the end of the day I cannot summon up any real passion to return to work the following day. Perhaps other employment options would fit me better, or maybe the grass isn't greener on the other side. I really don't know.

I'm still not sure what path my life will take regarding my career. I used to ask Sahana often to give me a sign of where I should go and what I should be doing. I still ask her, though less often, if I'm in the right career. It's normal to question one's role in the work force, but any feeling of uncertainty is only magnified after a great loss. Am I living the life I truly want to live?

"We must be willing to let go of the life we planned so as to have the life that is waiting for us."

– Joseph Campbell

From the first time I heard it, this quote really resonated with me. So, after a lot of deliberation in my mind and discussions with Priti, eleven months after our world changed forever, I decided to leave my job of 18 years. Not only was I leaving my co-workers, but I was leaving my second family. I was leaving the support structure that was helping me through this trying time. It was not an easy decision to make, but one that I needed to make to continue on my path of recovery. I needed a job that gave me a sense of purpose in the world. I needed to feel as if being alive made a difference in the world. I took a job for a government contractor involved in programs protecting the citizens of our country. Only time will tell if I am searching for something that does not exist. For me, it was worth the risk to try.

Additionally, on the side, I threw myself into a great distraction. I decided to get my real estate license so that I could be an agent part-time, while still working days as an aerospace engineer. After taking classes twice a week for two months, I received my license. I am so thankful for this process. This is probably the first time I've had an opportunity to take classes and not had the pressure of getting good grades or landing the perfect job. I took the classes more out of curiosity than anything else.

Prior to the tragedy, Priti was working full-time as a financial analyst for the pharmaceutical company in the area. After the tragedy, she decided to work only part-time, while also attending college, working towards getting her nursing degree. She is tantalizingly close to having her classes complete so she can apply to nursing school. To help fulfill this promise to Sahana, after a year of working part-time, Priti decided to quit her job entirely to focus solely on becoming an RN. This keeps Priti really busy, which is a good thing. While Sahana was in the hospital, Priti promised her that she would graduate from nursing school. So it makes classes a labor of love for Priti. She's good at helping people, and I know she will make an amazing nurse.

Along with attending classes, she is volunteering at a local hospital in patient services as well as a "cuddler" in the neonatal ICU (NICU). Though her volunteer duties don't have her practicing any form of medicine, she is gaining valuable experience working within the hospital environment. I know that Sahana is over the moon proud of her mommy for working towards her goal of helping people as a nurse.

For Priti to take on a volunteer job that has her involved with children was an easy decision. We have 11 nieces and nephews in our two families. In the days, weeks and months that followed our return to Virginia, they all visited us. It was hard at first seeing the kids play, but as they spent more time with us, the more we both became comfortable with interacting with little children again. Those interactions gave Priti the foundation and confidence to continue to pursue her promise to Sahana of becoming a pediatric nurse.

CHAPTER FOURTEEN – Visiting.

Mid-July following Sahana's death, we had a family member in the hospital. This was the first time I've been to a hospital since we'd been in Savannah. I didn't expect the feelings that ambushed me once within the hospital walls. I honestly thought I would be fine, just another visit to a hospital. Even getting out in the parking lot, I began to feel something come over me. I shrugged off the sensation as we made our way into the hospital. As I passed through the hospital entrance I realized that I wasn't fine, I wasn't fine at all. My mother noticed the change in me almost immediately.

As I explained to her that this was my first time visiting a hospital since Sahana had passed away, the realization struck my family as well. We exited the elevator on the second floor, each step down the hall causing emotions to build. With only 20 feet left to the hospital room we were meant to visit, I broke down in tears. I attempted to pull myself together long enough to enter the room quickly, pay my respects to the family and leave. The entire time within the hospital room was only about 20 seconds. Back in the hospital hallway, the world of medicine going on around me, I was able to compose myself. My family was very understanding of my emotional state, so for the rest of my time visiting the hospital I waited in a common sitting area for my family. I had overestimated how much I had actually recovered.

About a month after the accident I visited Sahana's daycare, Bean Tree Learning Center. Walking into this place that I had been to countless times, was much harder than I'd anticipated. Everything looked so normal, just like it had only a month earlier, but for me the entire world had changed. The staff at the learning center had fallen head over heels for Sahana's infectious personality. After the tragedy they met with me, bringing out their emotions at losing her spark. I laid eyes on Sahana's school pictures, so beautiful, my perfect baby girl. It wasn't easy for us to go to her daycare, but it was something that we had to do not only for ourselves but for her amazing

teachers as well.

CHAPTER FIFTEEN – Birthday Celebration.

August 15, 2014. On the day of Sahana's first birthday Priti wanted to separate the remembrance into two parts. We wanted some time to ourselves alone with Sahana before the rest of the family came to town. We started out our morning as we did every morning talking to Sahana, and on this day we wished her a Happy Birthday. Then together we went downstairs to watch the compilation video of our sweet little monkey. This time watching the images of her flash across the screen felt different. Somehow on this day it was harder to watch. I was more consumed with the feeling of wanting her there to share the moments we had planned. I'd gone to the local grocery store and bought a beautiful cupcake with a colorful butterfly on it, Sahana would love such a sweet and pretty cupcake. After watching the video, we took the butterfly cupcake and a picture of Sahana and set them on the kitchen counter and lit a number "1" candle on top of the cupcake. Together we sang Happy Birthday, or tried to. I didn't realize how difficult this would be. As we began to sing, both of us wept, but managed to struggle through the entire song.

The night before, Priti had baked some cookies in preparation for the remembrance. We took the cookies (along with a card explaining Sahana's story) to the local fire station as a token of our gratitude for everything they do for our community. It was because of the skilled EMT's in Savannah that Sahana's life was prolonged as much as it was. Since we weren't able to make it back to Savannah, we wanted to pay it forward to our local fire station, who save countless lives day after day. They were all very thankful for the delicious cookies Priti had made especially for them.

We then went to the hospital where Sahana was born and donated a collection of toys, clothes and a homemade blanket. We hadn't been back to the hospital since Sahana was born, but during our visit now, we had to explain why we were making the donation. It was tough to explain everything. The nurse who'd received us began to cry as we talked, which caused us to become misty-eyed along with her. It was an emotional trip to the hospital, standing in the building which had brought us our greatest miracle. We left knowing the visit was a good thing and confident that our little miracle was happy watching over us.

After our visit to the fire station and the hospital, our family began to arrive. We welcomed our family and close friends into our home for a celebration of life. It was an amazing summer day. The sky was a spectacular shade of blue without a cloud in sight. It was warm, and a gentle breeze played throughout the air. Together we ate some food and shared our favorite memories of Sahana, remembering the wondrous life she'd lived to the fullest. Together we all gathered around the birthday cake Priti had made and sang Happy Birthday to Sahana. Even though it was the second time Priti and I had sung, it wasn't any easier this time. We broke down at the same point we had the first time.

As a large family, we sat in front of our TV and watched Sahana's compilation video. For the rest of family and friends, it would be the first time they'd seen it. For Priti and me, we've watched the video a million times and are still filled with the same emotions. Looking around watching our family as they watched the video, it was obvious that the images affected them the same way it did us.

We had asked everyone who came to bring a present, as if they were giving it to Sahana on her birthday. The idea was to collect all of the presents and donate them to children in need. We ended up donating them to the Children's Hospital in Washington, DC. It was a wonderful way of sharing Sahana's love for toys and laughter with other children. We knew that Sahana would like this very much.

We rounded out the day by having every person at the gathering write whatever they wanted to Sahana on a piece of paper. Each piece of paper was then tied to a balloon, with one balloon per person. As a group we walked to the path near our home, the sun shining warmly down upon us. Standing in a grassy open field, Priti and I thanked everyone for coming and sharing in the celebration of Sahana's life. Then we released the balloons into the gentle summer breeze. It was an amazing sight to watch all 30+ balloons twirl and dance across the brilliant blue sky.

CHAPTER SIXTEEN – Dublin, Ireland.

At the end of August 2014 I planned to take a trip to Europe with two of my best college friends. We'd all gone to Penn State together, and Penn State would be playing a regular season football game in Dublin against Central Florida University. All three of us are huge Penn State football fans, and so we'd booked this vacation the previous year.

Priti and I'd talked about it, discussing whether I should still go. After some talking, we agreed that it would be good for me to get away for a few days. I was excited to go; watching football with my friends was always enjoyable, but watching it in Dublin would put it over the top. Along with my excitement came a little dose of apprehension. I wasn't exactly sure how I would react emotionally on the trip, but seeing that it was with two of my closest friends, I figured it would be okay.

While overseas, my buddy and I decided to take a side trip to London, our first stop upon landing in Europe, since neither of us had ever been. It was a very brief trip, only long enough to see some major sites, enjoy some great food and kick back with a few drinks at a couple of bars. In total we were in London for two days. From there we were off to Dublin, meeting up with our third friend to enjoy all that Dublin had to offer. The three of us immersed ourselves completely in the culture, getting to know the locals in some amazing pubs along busy brick streets dotted with walkers. During our time in Ireland we visited the Guinness factory on James Street, the Old Jameson Distillery, and The Brazen Head (the oldest pub in Ireland) which overlooks the river Liffey. We walked through the corridors of Trinity College, marveling at the beautiful architecture and marble statues. The game itself was filled with excitement. Penn State blew a lead early on, but we ended up winning on a last second field goal.

The trip, of course, was bittersweet, serving as a distraction from what was going on in my "real life" by allowing me to spend quality time on an adventure with friends. During this time I talked to my friends about how Priti and I were doing, and opening up felt good. Yet during my days in Europe – enjoying the sights, laughing with my friends – I felt guilty. With such a tragic loss and so many people in pain, was it okay for me to be enjoying myself? At moments I would find myself overcome with sadness and would have to slip away to find somewhere I could be alone. My friends understood, giving me space, if I needed it, to compose my thoughts.

The trip lasted six days. I would be able to concentrate clearly for a few hours, but then I would need some privacy to regroup. The trip was fun, the company was great, but towards the end of the trip I looked forward to getting home to Priti. Although she had my parents to keep her company, I knew she was struggling, and I longed to be by her side. Once the plane touched down in Virginia, it was back to reality.

CHAPTER SEVENTEEN – Gizmo.

We'd always talked about getting a family pet, a dog. It's one of those things that you say you will start discussing in six months, then six months pass and you put it off for another six months. The topic just keeps getting kicked down the line until before you know it, several years have passed. After my trip to London and Dublin, Priti wanted to think seriously about getting a dog. We both needed something to take care, to nurture, and a dog would provide that for us. Getting a dog was either going to be a huge success or an epic failure. Over the past few years we'd researched what type of dog to get – now all we needed to do was find the right breeder, which we accomplished in September 2014, bringing home the newest member of our family, Gizmo. Named after the character in the 80's movie "Gremlins," a movie I love, our Gizmo is a Havanese.

Professionals are beginning to realize just how instrumental dogs can be in helping a person overcome severe trauma, including that overwhelming anxiety reaction, posttraumatic stress disorder, which we both had. Dogs, who are capable of bringing companionship and love into a home, are used to treat all types of PTSD. Although neither Priti nor I has been formally diagnosed with PTSD, we knew soon after the tragedy that each of us was dealing with it. We avoided certain places that reminded us of the physical setting of the accident. We avoided people for a while, not wanting to have conversations about what happened. We felt panic in certain situations such as around balconies and high places in general, and in hospitals.

Gizmo was definitely one of the best ideas we had after the accident. He helps out a lot with our PTSD. Neither of us understood what it meant to be a dog owner before we got him, but we get it now. He is a full-fledged member of our family: in our eyes he is a four-legged child. When we walk through the door, he is so happy to see us. Wherever we go, he is our adorable shadow tagging alongside. He loves us unconditionally, without question or demand. He's a quiet little guy, hardly ever barking, and overall very low maintenance. Both of us are recovering much more quickly because he is with us.

CHAPTER EIGHTEEN – Feelings.

I simply can't say this enough: family is everything. In these times of deepest sorrow extended family would drive over three hours to visit with us, some only staying for an hour before returning home. They wanted us to know that even in our saddest moments, they were there to support us. They wanted to share their support, while also giving us our privacy to grieve. We appreciated each of these people for taking the time to be there for us.

Guilt can sneak into your subconscious and attack before you realize it. Enjoying dinner at a restaurant with Priti and our friends can make me feel guilty. Taking in a movie on a Sunday afternoon makes me feel guilty. Doing things I enjoy, it all makes me feel guilty. I know that Sahana wants her mommy and me to be happy, but feeling happy makes it seem as if we have gone on without Sahana. The truth, though, is that neither we nor anyone else who met her will ever forget

Sahana. She lives on in the hearts of every person she touched in her nine months of life. Once in a while, with laughter and joy, comes a feeling that we have let her go, even though letting go is never a possibility.

Sadness is a phantom in the night. It creeps up on you when you least expect it. After an uneventful day at work, the sadness can stab me like a knife with the realization Sahana won't be there to greet me when I get home. Grabbing a cup of coffee at Dunkin' Donuts, a little two-year-old girl with pigtails comes in. This stops me cold, and I think, "Sahana could have been that age." A song, a picture, a commercial on TV... it comes out of nowhere.

The worst days that bleed into the worst nights happen after extended time spent with family and friends. We are so lucky to be surrounded by wonderful people in our lives, but those wonderful people have wonderful children, and those wonderful children serve to remind me of the wonderful

daughter we lost. The days spent with family and friends, I

want so badly for Sahana to share in those moments with us. I

want her to be the little girl with chocolate ice cream on her

cheeks swinging on the playground. I want to be the parent

saying, "Monkey! Don't climb too high! You don't want to slip

and bonk your nose." I want to be the one to put a Band-Aid

on the skinned knee. Days with friends and family usually

remind me that those times with Sahana will never come

again.

Tears so often come out of nowhere and are unstoppable

when they do come. When Priti cried, as Holly advised, I let

her. Sometimes I would rush to her side, holding her against

me or taking her hand, comforting her with touch until the

tears subsided and her breathing steadied. Other times I

would wait quietly as she cried, not rushing to touch her. I did

this not because I didn't want to console her, but because I

love my wife greatly and seeing her in pain breaks my heart.

The times when I didn't go to her side were to allow her a private moment to express the built-up emotion that needed release.

Just how I helped Priti through her expressions of pain depended on what had triggered the tears. Many times I found myself feeling helpless to calm her breaking heart. I searched for magical words to lessen her pain, but found only blankness in my mind. So I did the only thing I could do, I stood by her side physically and emotionally. As long as I live, Priti will never have to be alone, and I will be her strength on days her own strength is a little shaky.

Although Priti wasn't the only one who cried, I mainly did so in private – when I was alone with my thoughts in the shower I would sob. When I cried alone, I wouldn't be consoled, and I didn't want to be consoled. I wanted to embrace my emotions and my thoughts and allow the release of the emotional pressure through tears. I wanted to be sad, angry and lost without worrying about who was watching me break down. Men believe they are the strong ones, providing stability to those around us. But sometimes even the strong crack.

As time went on we also developed questions regarding our home and its unavoidable association with Sahana. People asked, "Will you stay or will you sell?" – a question which sent us on endless rounds of soul searching. It made some sense to sell the house and get a fresh start in a new area, do something different in order to move forward.

But as time passed, the nature of our talks changed. Sahana is attached to our home, it is her home. She's a little girl who lived her life inside these walls. She is drawn to the house, her spirit still lives within this space. So for right now, at least, this is where we will stay.

Along with staying in Sahana's home, our home, we are staying within our community. Our neighborhood is a safe place filled with amazing people and wonderful relationships. We could move, sure, but then we would gamble on ever finding a place that feels this inviting. Maybe in the future, moving will be the right thing to do. Right now we choose to stay.

CHAPTER NINETEEN – Reconnecting with Valerie.

On October 26, 2015 we reconnected with Valerie. Priti was nervous about meeting with her. In the months since the accident I had been the one corresponding with Valerie via email. During those months so near in time to the accident, Priti was in no condition to communicate directly with Valerie. She did, however, read all the emails between Valerie and me. The day of the meeting Priti was still a little bit nervous. I wasn't, but I did anticipate Valerie's nervousness. The goal of our meeting was twofold: to thank Valerie in person and to help the three of us move forward.

Valerie had suffered through the accident as well. The three of us coming together was a great opportunity to discuss our healing and provide comfort to one another. The meeting went well, and I feel as if we each walked away with a small amount of closure. As a gift for Valerie, we framed a picture of Sahana with a thank-you note on the back. We wanted her to know how grateful our family is for everything she did on that tragic day. Valerie was there for Sahana, without being asked, because she is a kind-hearted person. There are not enough *thank you*'s in the world for all she did in those moments.

CHAPTER TWENTY – Family Vacation and Holidays.

Over the summer, Priti's family took a family vacation to Ocean City, Maryland. Priti and I decided we felt good enough to venture out on this family vacation. For the most part this trip was very relaxing, neither one of us experiencing extreme highs or lows. It was nice to be with family and enjoy ourselves a little bit again. It was on this trip that Priti and I learned of our aversion to heights, that we didn't feel comfortable going out on the balcony. The thought of Sahana was too overwhelming.

I also learned that we weren't doing as well as we thought we were. It hit me the evening of July 4th, sitting at the condo watching the fireworks that Sahana wasn't with us. That sadness only grew when we returned home to an empty house. This was one of Priti's lowest points since our first few days home from Savannah without Sahana. Out of nowhere an overwhelming feeling of emptiness came over both of us.

My family had planned an Ocean City, New Jersey vacation later in the summer as well, originally scheduled for the past June, but now for early August. This Ocean City is a wonderful beach town that is family- and child-friendly. Kids were everywhere running around, playing, having fun with their friends and family. There were moments when those laughing happy children were heartbreaking for us, turning a magnifying glass on the missing part of our family. In Indian tradition, August brings the Hindu festival called Raksha Bandhan (where sisters and brothers celebrate the love between them), which was incredibly sad for us. We knew Sahana should have taken part in this tradition. She would have done this for her cousins while on vacation here. The sadness we felt was rich and heavy.

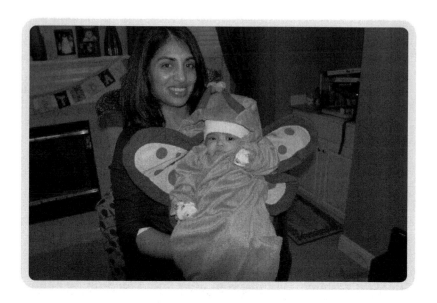

Halloween is such a playful and exciting time for most families, but Halloween 2014 only served to remind us of what was missing. The Halloween before, at only two-and-a-half months old, Sahana had been dressed up as a butterfly. She was one of the cutest things I had ever seen. This year, however, Priti and I hid away behind a darkened doorstep. Front light off, we avoided the laughing boys and girls dressed up as princesses and superheroes. I never imagined Halloween could bring me to tears, but the thought that Sahana wasn't one of those giggly kitty cats or pumpkins broke my heart.

We decided to visit my cousin's home to get away from the stillness of our house. I couldn't fight back the burning behind my eyes when I saw all the children dancing from house to house, giant smiles adorning their faces. I wanted to do that, I wanted it so badly, my chest ached as if it would burst.

For us all holidays are tough, especially around Christmas. I went to Target during the holidays to pick up some small items, and my eyes fell on the Christmas decorations. The aisles were filled with children roaming up and down, excitedly pointing out items to their parents. I know Sahana would have loved to see the Christmas decorations and lights. She liked things that twinkled, that sparkled brightly like her smile. I know, going forward, holidays will be tough to maneuver.

CHAPTER TWENTY-ONE – Savannah after the Tragedy.

Priti and I decided to make the trip back to Savannah for Sahana's Remembrance Ceremony. The day of the Remembrance Ceremony, November 16, 2014, was filled with intense anticipation. I was eager to begin my day, waking before my brother and Priti. I took a shower to clear my head and spent time packing and talking to Sahana about the day until everyone else woke up. I asked her to show us a sign that she was with us today as a city remembered her.

Surprisingly, driving to Savannah was better than I had expected. My brother and I took turns driving, and everyone made small talk throughout the drive. As we got closer to Savannah, a wave of emotion washed over me. I watched the highway signs counting down the miles to Savannah... Savannah 90 miles.....Savannah 50 miles...... Savannah 20 miles. I tried to fight back the tears, but finally they just fell down my face. We were almost back to a city that had brought us so much joy and so much unspeakable sadness.

Our last visit to Savannah with Sahana had been so wonderful. On this drive, I remembered all the people admiring our daughter's beauty and personality. I smiled, thinking about feeding her breakfast on her green Bumbo floor seat in the lounge, the joy we felt walking through the parks on such a beautiful early summer day. Chatting with a family, very much like our own, who had made the move to Savannah. It was a happy remembrance, but then the sadness would wash back over me. These times were worse when my brother drove, allowing me entirely too much time alone with my own thoughts, circulating through happy, sad and angry. No matter the emotions or the memories, thinking is therapeutic for me. In thinking I remember, and each time I remember I know her memory is still living strong.

After we arrived we found ourselves strolling through the beautiful city as we had done two times before. Not that we had forgotten, but in these moments the city reminded us of all its promise. We walked through the squares remembering how we had fallen in love with the city the first time we laid eyes on it. I wanted to know how I would react if I once again lost myself on the Savannah streets, and the answer came through loud and clear: This could still be our city. Sahana, our angel, had brought us here. She'd guided us to Savannah because of the beauty, the people, and because of her. During our walk my hands shook from raw emotion, but I was not overcome with sadness. I felt hope.

We journeyed to the waterfront area where there are laid-brick sidewalks, old cobblestone roads, quaint shops and restaurants with delicious cuisine. Seeing the waterfront reminded me of our bringing Sahana here and how everyone we passed commented on her cuteness. I stood quietly, overlooking the water, in the spot where I had last held her in my arms. I embraced the memory of us getting her name written in wire from a street vendor. We went into a souvenir shop where my brother picked up an item for his daughter, and right next to it we saw a wooden plaque with the words, "You are my sunshine." In the hospital Priti would sing that song nonstop while Sahana lay sleeping. It was then that we knew, Sahana was with us on this trip to Savannah as well.

We decided to visit the hotel where our lives changed forever, for reasons I cannot explain. All I know is I felt drawn to visit the place where she had fallen. I wasn't sure if Priti would be up to it, but she wanted to join me, even though she felt strong emotions at the thought of being in that place again. It only took a few steps into the lobby before Priti was overcome, tears washing her face. I took my amazing wife in my arms and held her as tightly as I could. She looked up at the balcony where Sahana had fallen and surveyed the floor where she had come to rest. Standing there, my wife against my chest, I felt numb. You see, I'd already had the opportunity to survey the hotel, the night of the accident when I had returned for the car. Standing in the lobby then, I think a part of me knew that Sahana wasn't going to make it. This visit, though, I felt something different. I felt amazed at our daughter's strength; it was incredible that she had even survived the fall and lived for three more days. Strength. When I think of her, I think of her incredible strength.

Later we visited the hospital PICU. We were able again to see the place where Sahana spent her last three days. Although it was an emotional experience, we were both surprised that it wasn't as bad as we had anticipated. I could feel the weight of the situation weighing me down, but it was bearable. Perhaps in that moment Sahana was offering me some of her unfaltering strength. It was amazing to see the wonderful nursing staff who had taken such wonderful care of Sahana during her time in the hospital. Nurses told us that they still think about Sahana and pray for us, which we greatly appreciate. It was truly wonderful to be with these people, who had cared for us all in one way or another, once again. Seeing the other nurses with whom we had connected and who had taken care of Sahana was great. Priti gave them a note thanking them for everything they had done. She also gave them a photo of Sahana. That picture of Sahana will remain on display in the PICU ward.

The Remembrance Ceremony was at Wesley Gardens, a magical and beautiful place, the perfect place to remember the one who left us too soon. The ceremony took place in two parts, one indoors and the other outdoors. The indoor ceremony had a seating area for all of the families, with a podium for speakers and a big screen on the side. There were about 30 or so people in attendance this day. Members of the hospital staff and the chaplain said a few words, thanking everyone for coming and explaining why they felt it important to have this ceremony. On the big screen began a slideshow of pictures dating back to 2012, images of children who had passed away during their stay at the hospital. Each child held his or her own space on a slide with their birthday and the date they passed away. My heart broke a little more with each passing slide, there were so many children's lives lost, many of them newborns. Then it was time for Sahana's slide. I could do nothing but cry. Seeing her pictures with the birthdate and date of passing brought back the pain. I missed my monkey.

The second part of the ceremony took place on a dock outside overlooking a water inlet. It was a very peaceful setting with open air and water, not many houses in sight. The staff handed out flowers to each of us. The chaplain read a poem while a guitarist played soft music. At the end, we each had moments to ourselves and then threw our flowers into the water. Afterwards, we stood there and watched the flowers float away. The ceremony itself lasted about two hours. This ceremony is held every year to remember these children, now angels. I believe that we will make every effort to return for the ceremony each year.

CHAPTER TWENTY-TWO – Taking Sahana to India.

We decided to spread Sahana's ashes in India over the Christmas holidays. I'd looked into doing this somewhere in the United States, but I couldn't find a place that seemed perfect. Together, Priti and I decided that India seemed like the right place for Sahana. India was a place we had always planned to visit with our daughter. Since Sahana had never been there, this would be our way of taking her there. We would spread her ashes in water, preventing any evil spirits from latching onto her.

Bringing Sahana's ashes home was an emotional day. Since her cremation, her ashes had been kept at the funeral home, until we took them to India. As part of our Hindu culture we could not bring her ashes into our home, which is why they remained safely at the funeral home. The day before we left for India, my brother went to pick up her ashes. Later that afternoon we picked up the ashes from my brother's home where they were sealed tightly in a little box. Priti held the ashes in her lap, and I placed a hand on the box as we drove home in silence. When we finally got home, I put the car in park, and we took turns holding the box that held her ashes. I couldn't stop crying. For me, it felt like the first day we got home from Savannah without Sahana. For the rest of the day, Priti and I both were in the saddest of moods.

The flights to India were thankfully uneventful, no turbulence, just smooth flights. Sahana's ashes were held securely in her mother's arms the entire flight, unless they had to be stowed away for certain parts of the flight. We were just a little nervous about getting through customs with her ashes and sometimes overwhelmed with anticipation about finally getting to India. We both felt at ease for the most part, although since Priti was holding Sahana's ashes the whole time, she would occasionally have memories trickle in and give her a little uneasiness.

When we arrived in Mumbai and moved into the customs lines, something amazing happened. We'd arrived in the afternoon, and so the lines at customs were minimal. There were about 20 lines, and all were open, with maybe one or two families in each. We stepped into a line that had only one other family in it. About two minutes later another family arrived with two daughters. They could have easily picked any of the 20 lines to enter, but they picked the one we stood in. Then the mom of the family behind us called out her daughter's name....Sahana! I did a double take the first time I heard it, thinking certainly I must have misheard. The second time she said her daughter's name, Priti heard it as well, and then I knew I had heard it right the first time. We both smiled. Our Sahana was giving us a sign that she was with us on this trip, as she had been on all our trips before. Sahana is not a common Indian name, and to have this family pick our line at that moment could not have been just a random act.

10:00 a.m. in Chandod, India. The morning of the ceremony greeted me with anxiety. For over six months I had waited for this day – December 23, 2014 – to lay our little girl to rest. Freeing her to be at peace.

The village of Chandod lies in the state of Gujarat about 60 km south of where my family was staying in India. It's the site where three holy rivers meet: the Narmada, the Orsang and the Saraswati. The Narmada and Orsang rivers are physical rivers, while the Saraswati River is imaginary (it protrudes from the earth upwards). We knew this was the ideal place for Sahana.

Priti, my parents and I attended to Sahana's Remembrance

Ceremony details. It was held in an open room near the river,

which was dedicated specifically to the ceremony. We opened

the box with Sahana's ashes and then spoke her name out

loud. The Priest asked how she died – we said by an accident.

How she died would dictate what type of ceremony he

performed. The Priest began the ceremony with a blessing.

We then opened the bag of ashes and poured them into a

ceremonial dish. This moment was surreal for us since this

was the first time we had actually seen her ashes. My eyes

welled with tears at the sight, the realness of the ashes on the

ceremonial dish. I thought, this is our Sahana's full body, it

now fits in this small bag.

The Priest recited prayers and advice during the entire

ceremony. I found my eyes filled with tears the entire time. I

felt nothing but the tears in my eyes and focused as hard as

possible on the Priest's words. Priti cried as the ceremony

continued. We poured a tablespoon of water on the ashes

three times; in the Hindu religion many religious ceremonial rituals are done in threes. Then we placed flowers in the ashes. Again, we poured a tablespoon of water on her ashes three times. Then we placed hay on her ashes, which signifies good wishes. We then poured a tablespoon of water on her ashes three times more. Then we said out loud all of the nicknames we had for Sahana:

Monkey. Giggle Monster. Slobber Monster. Monkey Pants. Bucca.

Saying each name out loud for her. Forcing tears to choke within my throat, because I felt as if I were talking directly to her as I spoke each name.

Everyone laid additional flowers on top of her ashes. We then made a donation to the Priest in Sahana's name. The ceremonial tray of ashes was then taken to the river where a boat waited. The boat took us out onto the water and to the site where the three holy rivers intersect. Taking turns, Priti

and I spread her ashes atop the water. When all of her ashes

had been spread, the boat brought us back to shore. To

signify the closing of the ceremony, I circled a holy tree three

times and brought the ceremonial tray back to the Priest.

CHAPTER TWENTY-THREE – Signs.

Day after day I see signs of Sahana everywhere. Walking, I see a beautiful white duck floating elegantly along the surface of a lake. It reminds me of a few days before the accident, during what I now think of as the "normal" time. Our backyard overlooks a sparkling lake. On this day at least ten brown ducks floated across the surface, but magically in the middle of all the brown feathers swam one white duck. We noticed that the white duck would be on the water one day but nowhere in sight the next. Ducks were also by Sahana's side in PICU since the hospital had given her a handmade quilt and a white duck Beanie Baby. Of all the Beanie Baby's they might have chosen, they gave her a white duck. I don't believe in coincidences. Everything happens for a reason.

Dragonflies appear in the most unsuspecting places; following me through a grocery store parking lot or dancing outside our windows at home. In many cultures a dragonfly symbolizes transformation. Dragonflies remind us of joy, like the indescribable joy of a daughter to her parents. Dragonflies can also mean wisdom and change; like the way Sahana gave her mother and me so much knowledge both in life and death.

Along with dragonflies, butterflies now hover around us. We see butterflies everywhere from random pictures to clothes on people in the streets.

Many times when I've been talking to Sahana, lights flip on and off with no earthly reason for them to do so. I remember a text message from Priti one afternoon explaining how she felt drawn to Sahana's room. Once in the room an overwhelming scent of Sahana filled the air. I can still picture the excited text message and the warmth I felt when reading it.

"She was here…I smelled her," Priti had written. My little girl was looking out for her amazing mommy.

We aren't the only ones feeling visits from Sahana. Sahana's "best friend" is a little girl named Laurel who lives in our neighborhood. On the day Sahana died, the best friend said Sahana's name for the first time. Now months later she constantly says Sahana's name. Best friends are a magical thing, and I believe that even in her afterlife Sahana visits her friend and watches over her.

I'm taken aback by buzzing and ringing in my ears at random times. From my readings of the afterlife, this phenomenon is our loved one's attempts to communicate with us. She has to lower her vibrational frequency to get to our level; it is Sahana's earthly way of trying to connect to us. I used to think nothing of this sound, but now I welcome it. When I do hear it,

I usually say "Hi, Sahana." I hear this buzzing and ringing typically one or two times a day.

The day we left for vacation, May 22, 2014, Priti saw a hearse. Looking back we wonder if this was a bout of mother's intuition. How often does one see a hearse during their day-to-day outings? Sahana was a little more needy and touchy feely the days leading up to the accident as well. Sahana seemed like she wanted to be held more than usual. When we held her, she would take her fingers and feel our faces and try and kiss us a little more than usual. Maybe this was in our minds, but she definitely seemed as if she wanted to touch us more.

Her temperament changed from comfortable in her stroller to being more of that child who wanted to be picked up. Was it due to all of the crowds at the street festival? Did she know something was going to happen? Only she knows. She was normally a low maintenance baby...but during her last hour she was a little more high maintenance in terms of needing our interactions.

One day Gizmo woke up suddenly from lying next to Sahana's toys in the corner of our family room. He rarely barks, but on this occasion he jumped up and didn't stop barking for about 90 seconds. Our quiet fur-ball literally barked the entire time. He jumped back and forth as though he saw something...he saw Sahana! ...he has done this now many times since we've gotten him. They say dogs can sense these things. I am a believer, and I think Gizmo is too.

On another occasion, Gizmo was laying down and resting next to Sahana's high chair in the kitchen. On that day, he got startled by something and jumped up and looked back at the high chair, then instinctively he walked backwards away from the high chair. What did he see? In my opinion he saw our little girl.

CHAPTER TWENTY-FOUR – New Beginnings.

When we came back from India, we started trying again for another baby. We've asked Sahana to bless us with another baby like her when she thinks we are ready. With all of the difficulties we had the first time around, my fear is that Sahana was our only opportunity to parent a child. However, through that fear I have faith. I'm not sure what the future has in store for Priti and myself, but I know whatever it is we will face it together. Priti, me, and our guardian angel.

In the process of writing this memoir, I told a friend to ask me what he wanted to know about my experience through this tragedy. He asked me a few really good questions.

Is Saumil still traumatized?

I don't believe I am, but I am still hurting. All I can know is that I am in a better place than I was the days following the accident. I will never be the same as when Sahana was still

alive, but I have come to terms with that. Time does help. It

just seems as if it takes a long time to get to the point where

your wounds are healing.

Will Sahana ever grow up?

In my mind, she will always be the nine-month-old

vibrant little girl who defined Priti and me. Whether it is in my

dreams or our next medium experience, she will always be the

girl who could not wait for daddy to pick her up at daycare.

Do you consider the burden you may be putting on Sahana

when you ask her to watch over people?

To be honest, I had never really thought about this

possible burden until my friend asked the question. It is similar

to the people who reach out to GOD for help.

I have to believe she is watching out for us and everyone she has touched every single day. I have to believe even though her body is gone, and that even though she has reincarnated to into another body, part of her is still with us, helping Priti and me on our journey.

Made in the USA
Middletown, DE
30 September 2015